"If you have a worrying problem, this book by Ben Ecl[...] carefully explains the inner workings of worry, and pre[...] that are derived from research-supported clinical inter[...]

—**Jonathan S. Abramowitz, PhD**, professor, and director of clinical training at the University of North Carolina at Chapel Hill

"Overflowing with both practical tools and illuminating perspectives on worry and anxiety in general, *Worrying Is Optional* seamlessly blends cognitive-behavioral with acceptance-based strategies. The book's unique transdiagnostic approach looks at the role of worry across the spectrum of anxiety disorders. Eckstein's confident voice guides the reader toward changing their relationship with worry, and cultivating a stronger connection to their core values. A comprehensive, powerful, and flexible guide!"

—**Chad LeJeune, PhD**, founding fellow of the Academy of Cognitive and Behavioral Therapies, and author of *The Worry Trap* and *"Pure O" OCD*

"I was initially worried I wouldn't have the time to read this book, but once I picked it up, the author's relatable and appropriately humorous tone led me to conclude that I did. *Worrying Is Optional* is a useful contribution to the anxiety-related self-help literature. It aptly makes the case that worrying never gets the job done that it promises to. Eckstein offers genuinely useful alternatives instead. Time well spent."

—**Jon Hershfield, LCMFT**, director of the Center for OCD and Anxiety at Sheppard Pratt, and coauthor of *The Mindfulness Workbook for OCD*

"Thank you to Ben Eckstein for providing a relatable and easy-to-understand guide to understanding and managing worry. At a time when worrying does NOT seem optional, Ben helps us to see that we have the power to control our worry with the use of clearly described strategies. I know I will be using and recommending this book."

—**Diane Davey, RN, MBA**, program director at the OCD Institute at McLean Hospital, and board member of the International OCD Foundation

"While worry can feel like it has a life of its own, the good news is that *you* can be the one in charge! Ben Eckstein educates us about how our minds work, and expertly weaves multiple ways to approach our worry differently. You don't have to be along for the ride with your worry. Learn how to get into the driver's seat and begin living your best life."

—**Jeff Szymanski, PhD**, founder of Getting to the Next Level Consulting, LLC; part-time clinical instructor at Harvard Medical School; and clinical associate at McLean Hospital

"Want to quiet those persistent worries? *Worrying Is Optional* is packed full of the powerful strategies we use in treatment, delivered to you in an easy-to-read, practical book. Written by a well-respected anxiety specialist and based on cutting-edge science, you'll find multiple ways to build your most effective plan. This book is truly an impressive accomplishment."

—**Reid Wilson, PhD**, psychologist, and author of *Stopping the Noise in Your Head*

"Worry is not the enemy, it's necessary and adaptive. Worry(ing), however, is ineffective and unhealthy. This is foundational to *Worrying Is Optional*, a thoughtfully crafted book for all anxiety disorders, offering comprehensive, evidence-based strategies and transforming our relationship with worry into a catalyst for personal growth. By addressing processes of worrying, rather than symptoms, Ben Eckstein compassionately teaches us that worrying about worries is truly optional and well within our control."

—**Josh Spitalnick, PhD, ABPP**, CEO/owner of Anxiety Specialists of Atlanta;
and author of the parenting guide, *Raising Resilience*

"*Worrying Is Optional* is an exceptional self-help workbook that is valuable to anyone struggling with worry. The gift of this beautiful book is that it teaches you how to accept what you can't control and live a meaningful life. Eckstein does a superb job exploring the function of worrying and other unhelpful covert mental behaviors. The exercises and tips throughout this book will help the reader be more aware of their unhelpful mental processes and responses, implement concrete strategies, and be more present in their lives. I look forward to sharing this wonderful resource with clients and friends!"

—**Marisa T. Mazza, PsyD**, psychologist, founder of choicetherapy, IOCDF BTTI
faculty, and author of *The ACT Workbook for OCD*

"What a delight to read! This metaphor-rich book empowers readers to dismantle worrying using tools from a wide evidence base. Eckstein acknowledges the complexity of how our brains can latch on to worries, and provides compassionate strategies to help people get out of the familiar rut of anxious patterns. Even better, he provides tools to help cultivate new patterns to live a purposeful and valued life."

—**Amy Mariaskin, PhD**, founding director of the Nashville OCD & Anxiety
Treatment Center, and author of *Thriving in Relationships When You Have OCD*

"Some people are prone to overthink or think a lot about important things, small matters, or day-to-day interactions. The challenge is that, as much as it feels natural to think and problem-solve things in our head, for some people, that ongoing thinking pattern keeps them stuck in a cycle of worry. Worry is a very common psychological struggle across many presentations and if it goes unchecked, it can be extremely debilitating in a person's life. In this book, Ben shows skills derived from different evidence-based approaches to tackle worry in a skillful, engaged, and actionable approach. Every chapter includes a specific skill to address different processes that maintain and perpetuate worry. This is a must-read book for anyone dealing with worry that wants to experience a joyful, vibrant, and meaningful life!"

—**Patricia E. Zurita Ona, PsyD**, author of *Acceptance and Commitment Skills for Perfectionism and High-Achieving Behaviors* and *Living Beyond OCD Using Acceptance and Commitment Therapy*

Worrying Is Optional

Break the Cycle of Anxiety & Rumination
That Keeps You Stuck

Ben Eckstein, LCSW

New Harbinger Publications, Inc.

NEW HARBINGER PUBLICATIONS is a registered trademark of New Harbinger Publications, Inc.

New Harbinger Publications is an employee-owned company.

Copyright © 2023 by Ben Eckstein
        New Harbinger Publications, Inc.
        5674 Shattuck Avenue
        Oakland, CA 94609
        www.newharbinger.com

All Rights Reserved

Cover design by Sara Christian

Acquired by Jennye Garibaldi

Edited by Joyce Wu

Library of Congress Cataloging-in-Publication Data on file

Printed in the United States of America

25   24   23

10   9   8   7   6   5   4   3   2   1   First Printing

For Becca

Contents

Foreword

Have you ever tried to talk yourself out of being afraid of something? For those of us who struggle with worry, rumination, or cognitive rituals in what has been called "pure O" OCD, this is a daily and exhausting task, one that can sometimes continue from dawn to dusk. It feels automatic, impossible to stop, never-ending. And we may have difficulty separating the practice of mental ritualizing from who we are. In fact, this notion is sometimes reinforced by mental health practitioners, who so often ask the question, "Are you a worrier?" The fact is you are not your worries. But it may be that you are stuck inside of them.

Why do we worry? And why does it often become so all-consuming? Generally speaking, humans don't like uncertainty. We like knowing the answers in order to reduce risk. We like our reality neatly categorized and sorted into neat little pockets, laid out before us like a bento box. We worry to reduce the anxiety and distress elicited by uncertainty and to provide a sense of control. Our brains tend to equate worrying about something with trying to solve it—even if that thing we are trying to solve isn't actually within our control. It will likely not surprise you that this kind of mental engagement is counterproductive, despite feeling compulsive or necessary. So why do we so often get stuck in it?

I once read a story of a tiger who had lived for many years in a tiny cage in which she spent her days circling, over and over. One day she was rescued and released into a vast green field in a wild animal sanctuary. Upon entering that new, unexplored meadow, she promptly found a corner and began circling again in the same dimensions as her cage. Worry, rumination, and cognitive rituals can feel like that: a necessary activity that gives us some semblance of control in our lives, in the absence of anything else we've discovered that might work. An important question to ask here is, *At what cost?* For the tiger, it was a potentially beautiful life that lay inaccessible, undiscovered.

For those of us who struggle with worry, we often try to think ourselves out of it. We use logic; we remind ourselves that our overconcern and rumination doesn't make sense, and wonder what's wrong with us that these insights don't ever seem to lead to meaningful change. But talking ourselves out of worry is a fool's errand. We need to look no further than our own stuckness for data to support that conclusion. What does work, however, involves two perhaps novel ideas. First, anxiety is not our enemy—but how we respond to it can be. Second, we can think about worry as a *behavior* in which we engage rather than something that happens to us, or something we are victims of, or "just who we are."

Worrying Is Optional by Ben Eckstein, a seasoned clinician with years of experience working with chronic worriers, OCD sufferers, and ruminators, offers an elegant, comprehensive, and process-based set of tools to help sufferers break the cycle of worry. Unlike so many other books, he delves deep into the *how* to practice exposure and response prevention (ERP) effectively with mental avoidance behaviors like rituals, worry, and rumination.

In clear and accessible language, this book addresses the worrying functionally, as a *process* rather than an outcome, making a clear distinction between a triggering thought and the ensuing, volitional activity of worrying. Using clear examples and engaging and effective exercises, the author provides a new perspective on the nature of worrying, rumination, and cognitive rituals, all of which share the same functional characteristics and can be addressed the same way.

This book is divided into four parts. Part 1 helps motivate readers to tackle worry by clarifying how it *works*, normalizing how it arises, undermining it as a control strategy, and describing it as a habit that, with practice, can be changed over time. Part 2 assists readers in developing a different relationship to anxiety and worry—one that is less adversarial and more workable. Integrating strategies from cognitive behavior therapy (CBT), acceptance and commitment therapy (ACT), and inference-based therapy (IBT), readers begin to shape foundational skills that will help them effectively use the evidence-based approach described in part 3, namely exposure and response prevention.

Part 3 provides readers with clear, actionable strategies to stop worrying. It describes specific responses to worry that can be accurately named, labeled, and therefore shaped—awareness, attention, and engagement. Readers learn when they might interact with these in problematic ways, and then are offered clear alternatives to shift these habits to break free from the cycle of rumination. Part 4 fosters self-compassion, willingness to practice the skills they have learned in previous sections imperfectly, with a heavy dose of kindness.

If you consider yourself a worrier and are holding this book in your hands, you are lucky indeed. If you make your way through it thoughtfully, remaining open to the ideas inside—and perhaps more importantly, by practicing them systematically, whether on your own or with a clinician—you will make significant headway out of the worry trap that's been keeping you stuck for so long. I encourage you to take your time. Don't give up. Lean into what you find in these pages. Let the practices lead you into that vast, green meadow, full of sunlight. Let the words in these pages help you turn uncertainty into beautiful, exquisitely joyful possibility.

Introduction

I decided to write this book because worrying is one of the most common problems that clients bring to my office. They think too much and they don't like it. Each person's version of anxiety and worry is a bit different. Each has its own texture and hue, comprising a litany of thoughts, feelings, beliefs, and sensations. This pattern of unhelpful thinking is trans-diagnostic. It shows up in obsessive-compulsive disorder (OCD) and generalized anxiety disorder (GAD). It's in social anxiety and post-traumatic stress disorder (PTSD), panic disorder and depression. So many of the mental health problems that my clients struggle with involve this same style of perseverative thinking.

Our cognitive inner lives can very easily become intertwined with our actual lives, coloring and informing how we experience the world. Anxiety and worry can start to feel so fundamental to who we are that sometimes we can forget to examine all of the different moving parts. The task of looking under the mental hood can feel daunting. This book will be a guide to examine how *your* anxiety and worry function, how they are maintained and perpetuated.

Like worry itself, this book is intentionally transdiagnostic. The ideas and skills contained here can be applied to any number of iterations of unhelpful thinking. While diagnosis can be a useful tool in many instances, it is very frequently a mere collection of symptoms. And symptoms are not always helpful for us. They're the byproduct—the external manifestation of another process that's a bit harder to see. If you go to the doctor with a fever, you don't get diagnosed with "fever disorder;" they try to figure out what's happening in your body to create that fever. They recognize that treating the symptom will only get you so far if you can't also tap into what's causing it.

In 2002, Billy Beane, the general manager of the Oakland Athletics, became known for an unorthodox approach to baseball. As popularized by the book and movie *Moneyball*, he was able to wrangle success out of a small payroll by using different metrics and statistics. He realized that some of the tools being used by the old guard of baseball were actually not that useful. Twenty-plus years later, baseball teams use statistics even more advanced than Beane's. They don't care about the output (the number of homeruns or hits); they care about the underlying metrics—the launch angle of the ball, the exit velocity off the bat, calculations that account for luck or predict expected outcomes. They've recognized that the output was merely a rough estimate, a loose correlation; for greater precision, they needed to go beyond these observable indicators and look at the mechanisms actually driving the outcomes.

Instead of symptoms, we're going to be looking at processes. What are the underlying processes that drive anxiety and worry? Are worries being perpetuated by behavioral reinforcement? Are they driven by an intolerance of uncertainty, faulty beliefs, or errors in reasoning? Are worries amplified by immersion in your imagination or fusion with your thoughts? Have you become so accustomed to operating in this way that it's now automatic or habitual?

As we expand on these aspects of anxiety and worry, you'll want to pay attention to the parts that resonate with you. Dismantling worry requires that we see it for what it is—that we understand what drives it and keeps it going. Worry is often composed of the same ingredients from person to person, but the precise recipe—the proportions of one ingredient or another—will vary. You'll need to know your unique blend. Rather than seeing the outcome—an anxious or worried person—take the time to examine the mechanisms that are at play. Once you understand the mechanisms, you'll be able to build and apply skills tailored to your own anxiety special sauce.

How to Make the Most of This Book

This book is broken down into several sections, each aiming to dismantle worry from a different angle.

In the first section, we'll focus on the nature of worry, helping you understand how anxiety works so that you can plan your approach and learn to respond more effectively. Anxiety is not the enemy—it's useful and adaptive—but you need to have a thorough grasp of how it works to prevent your worry from straying into unhelpful territory.

In the second section, we'll focus on challenging your relationship to anxiety and worry. You may have beliefs about worry—that it's beneficial, productive, or necessary—that contribute to your problem. You may find yourself mired in doubt, attending to a myriad of what-ifs and remote possibilities rather than forging a more solid foundation of trust in yourself. Your meta-awareness—that ability to be at the helm of your mind, observing and making conscious choices about how to interact with your internal experiences—will be pivotal as you start to develop new ways of relating to your thoughts, learning new approaches that will no longer maintain anxiety and worry.

In the third section, we'll use a behavioral lens to develop strategies to break the cycle of worry. By removing the components that reinforce and perpetuate worry and anxiety, you can extinguish these habits and learn new approaches to manage the chatter in your mind. Rather than avoiding painful or anxious thoughts, you'll learn to disengage from worry by strengthening your attention muscle and building skills to defuse from unhelpful thinking patterns.

The final section does a bit of reverse engineering: learning from the characteristics of non-worriers to establish a blueprint of how you can build a life less consumed by worry.

These approaches draw from several different treatment modalities. While there are several evidence-based treatments for anxiety, no single treatment has ever been shown to be effective for 100 percent of people. As useful as each model can be, they are all incomplete. They're tailored to address a particular "active ingredient" in anxiety. For example, exposure-based models might do wonders to address fear conditioning, but little to address the aspect of your worry that's driven by unhelpful beliefs about anxiety. Similarly, cognitive approaches might help you learn to relate to your anxiety differently, but without adding some concrete tools to help you disengage from worrying, this understanding and insight will only get you so far. Maybe you happen to be the unicorn whose worry can be boiled down to one specific mechanism, but I'm willing to bet that your worry is a bit more complicated. It's probably maintained by several factors, and it will require a more nuanced approach that can account for your individual complexity.

Remember, none of these methods are a "cure" for worry. They're tools and skills to help you live a life in which worry does not control you. They're a blueprint for a new approach to your internal experience— strategies to navigate the anxiety and incessant thoughts muddying your mind and preventing you from being present in your life. These skills will not transform you into a person oblivious to risk. You won't walk away without a care in the world. I can't just make you "chill." But I can offer you strategies that will enable you to relate to your cares and worries in a way where they no longer control your life. Let's get started!

PART I

Understanding
Worry

CHAPTER ONE

What Is Worry?

When we try to pick out anything by itself, we find it hitched to everything else in the Universe.

—John Muir, *My First Summer in the Sierra*

Many people come to my office hoping that I'll have the secret cure for their anxiety, and I suspect that many people will buy this book with that same hope. But I'm not in the business of making anxiety or worry go away. If you're someone struggling with these problems, the first thing you need to know is that you won't get better until you change your goal from getting rid of anxiety to learning to coexist with it more effectively. Anxiety is not bad. In fact, it's incredibly helpful and necessary. Without it, quite simply, we'd all die. We need it to alert us to danger and to prevent us from walking into traffic. It's a key part of our brain's system to detect threats and keep us safe. But for some people, likely *you* given that you are reading a book called *Worrying Is Optional*, this anxiety system can get a little wonky. Thoughts get bigger, more persistent, and harder to wrangle into our control. As a result of all those overgrown anxious thoughts, feelings often get more intense and they start showing up in places where they're unhelpful or where no threats exist. Maybe you've experienced this when you've anticipated a meeting at work, your mental rehearsal gradually building into dread. Or maybe it's when you've ago-nized over a decision, as your problem-solving snowballed into an endless rehashing of every detail and angle.

This system can get a bit unwieldy if you don't know how to tame it. In this book, we'll teach you how to regain control of your internal pro-cesses by equipping you with tools and skills so you can build a more adaptive response for when worry or anxiety show up in your life.

The Noun and the Verb

I don't want to be the grammar police, but there's an important distinc-tion that we need to make, right off the bat. There's worry and there's worrying. Worry, the noun, is a kind of thought that we all have from time to time. Worrying, the verb, is what happens when our minds are preoccupied with worry. The difference between these things may sound trivial, but it's essential to learn how to separate these two concepts.

Let's start with defining our terms in more detail: *worry* is an initial thought, the doubt that arises in your mind, the awareness of uncertainty. It shows up uninvited, unintentional, automatic. Your brain is responsible for generating these thoughts. That's part of its job: identify all of the pos-sible outcomes and scan for all of the potential threats. Remember, without your brain's automatic worry reaction, you'd be less likely to notice that car whizzing down the street even though you're in a cross-walk, or the subtle shift in body language letting you know that a friend is upset. At the same time, when your brain generates worries, it's not looking to analyze or refine these thoughts; it's just brainstorming. While some of these initial thoughts are helpful, a lot of them are garbage—mental spam filling up your mind's inbox. The initial thought is not in your control. You don't choose it. It just rises to the surface of your mind and then you get to decide what to do with it.

Worrying is a specific way that you respond to worry. You perceive that doubt, the random what-if that your brain has generated, and start to interact with it. That might mean directing your attention to it or actively engaging with it by analyzing. You try to solve it by eliminating uncertainty, mentally crunching numbers and scenarios into oblivion until every shred of doubt has been destroyed.

The key difference between worry and worrying is that worry is something that just happens; worrying is something that you choose to do. Worrying is active. Volitional. It may not always feel like it, but you're a participant and you have a role. Worry will happen whether you participate or not—you can't choose blissful ignorance of the world around you; your brain is going to keep taking in information, generating thoughts, and you're going to continue to be aware of them. But the next step, the worrying—that part you do have a say in. I know it can seem like your mind has been hijacked—that it's out of control. But that's what this book is about. It's about learning how to build the skills so you can establish agency over your mind. You don't have to be at the mercy of your thoughts.

All Worries Are Created Equal

We're going to be talking a lot about worrying in this book. And you may be wondering: "Does this apply to *my* brand of worry? Is there something different about my thoughts? If I have X diagnosis, does that change the approach?" Worrying is a transdiagnostic phenomenon. That means that aspects of worry show up in lots of different diagnoses. It comes in all different shapes and sizes.

Worry is usually most closely associated with GAD, which is best described as "excessive" worrying (I'll explain the quotation marks later). Folks with GAD deal with worry about everyday stressors, but it happens to such a degree that it starts to become impairing and distressing. GAD, however, is not the only diagnosis that involves perseverative thoughts or rumination—far from it.

The *obsessions* in OCD are repetitive, unwanted thoughts that cause distress. They're followed by *compulsions* that are intended to prevent or reduce that distress. For example, *I'm worried I'll get sick from touching that doorknob* (obsession), *so I'll go wash my hands* (compulsion). You're probably familiar with some of the tangible, observable compulsions such as hand-washing or checking, but OCD frequently involves mental compulsions as well. Like all compulsions, these mental efforts are intended to reduce distress or uncertainty. These could include things like rumination, mental review, thought-stopping, and many other more subtle mental processes. The OCD framework of obsessions and compulsions is functionally the same as the differentiation between worry and worrying. Obsessions and worry both evoke distress, while compulsions and worrying both functionally serve to reduce that distress.

But that's not all! In fact, every anxiety-related problem will involve some aspects of these mental processes. Phobias, social anxiety, panic disorder, PTSD—these diagnoses frequently involve rumination and other mental efforts to solve the problem of anxiety or uncertainty.

While these diagnoses may have different flavors, worrying is still worrying. The outward presentation and content of anxiety may vary, but the internal mechanisms at play still overlap. The process of mental examination is consistent across diagnoses and often fills a similar function, regardless of a particular diagnosis (or even if you don't meet the criteria for a diagnosis at all). If you have social anxiety, it may be that you get hooked by thoughts about social interactions or the potential judgment of others. If you have OCD, the kinds of thoughts that hook you may have to do with harm or morality or perfection. If GAD is your thing, you may get stuck on thoughts about everyday stressors or problems. Whatever the content, the problem remains the same—you struggle to disentangle yourself from these thoughts when you get hooked.

The Road to Worrying Is Paved with Good Intentions

Some people say that OCD differs from GAD in that compulsions are disproportionate and, at times, not meaningfully or logically connected to the fear. Essentially, compulsions don't always make sense. Checking a lock once? Sure. You might even catch an error once in a while. But checking ten times? Twenty times? Not so much. I've had plenty of clients tell me that they checked once and—lo and behold—the door was unlocked! But I've never had anyone tell me that they checked nine times and found the door locked, *but on the tenth time*, it was unlocked! That just doesn't make much sense. And that's one of the signature features of OCD: awareness that what you're doing to try to resolve your fears doesn't make sense but feeling like you have to do it anyway.

I would argue that GAD is no different. Let's say you have a big physics test coming up on Friday. You've struggled in physics and you really need to do well to salvage a decent grade for the class. You have three days until the test. If you want to maximize your chances of doing well on the test, should you a) study for the test, or b) worry about the test?

That's easy! It's obvious! Worrying might seem appealing; you have a very real problem staring you down. But will that increase your chances of doing well? No! Absolutely not. Worrying is not the same as studying. It's not effective. It accomplishes nothing. Like a compulsion, it's not meaningfully connected to the fear. It masquerades as something helpful, but it's not. It's like checking a lock ten times: it has its origin in something that is potentially useful, but it's been twisted and bent into something that has lost any semblance of utility. You're now just spinning your wheels, getting no closer to your goal, under the guise of doing something helpful.

This is the reason I say "excessive" worrying with quotation marks. Worrying, by definition, is excessive. It's unhelpful and ineffective. It's distinct from things like planning, problem-solving, reflecting, and so forth. Those things are all useful. "Excessive" worrying is sort of like saying "ATM machine"—the "machine" part is redundant. All worrying is excessive. If you're worrying, you've forsaken those effective tools that move you toward your goal and have instead started engaging in a behavior with a completely different goal—reducing distress. You've crossed the line from something useful into something unnecessary and no longer meaningfully related to your goal. Your actions have stopped advancing your cause, but you're still pouring energy into them anyway.

You may be saying to yourself, *But worrying has helped me!* You may be recalling a time when you worried and everything worked out; you felt better prepared or were glad that you had anticipated a possible outcome. I would suggest that you're probably conflating worrying with planning. You're mistaking worrying for the active ingredient, when really, it's just the filler. Worrying was the thing that accompanied the positive results, but it's not the thing that caused them. If you achieved your goal and were better prepared, chances are good that you did something effective to reach that goal. It wasn't because you turned it over and over in your head a thousand times; it was because you actively problem-solved and did something to help your cause.

It can be really difficult to tell when you've crossed a line, when you've veered from a useful tactic like planning into a superfluous mental churning. This line is often easiest to see once you've crossed it, when you're squarely on the other side—anxiety is ramping up, or you're beginning to notice that you've spent a lot of time on your problem but don't have much to show for it. The reality of most of the lines that we draw is that they're not precise. You can't possibly know the exact moment you shift from helpful to unhelpful, effective to ineffective. Instead, you're probably going to swerve back and forth across that line. When you're worrying, you're choosing to err on the side of caution. When in doubt, do more. Better to cross the line than risk not doing enough. Sacrifice efficiency for the pursuit of certainty.

The table below illustrates some of these lines, though of course the real-world application of this will be a bit messier.

Helpful	Unhelpful
Analysis; Problem-solving	Rumination; Fretting
Learning from past experiences; Reflection	Mental review; Mental checking
Planning; Hypothesizing	Needing to know with certainty; Mental rehearsal
Connecting with reality; Using logic and reasoning	Seeking reassurance

The Shapes of Worrying

One of the first steps in breaking free of worrying will be to identify it. You can't stop something if you can't see it. We'll continue to add more tools for building awareness as we go along, but let's start with simply identifying some of the mental processes implicated in worrying.

Worrying tends to be a bit of a catchall. It's an umbrella term that includes many different variations and methods of responding to worry. Don't be shy about identifying your particular brand of worrying—every single human being does every single one of these things sometimes. Before you do though, I want you to consider, briefly, a bit of political strategy: the use of human-interest stories in campaign speeches. You know the type: "I spoke to a family in West Virginia who lost their jobs when the coal mine closed," or "I met a young man who was working three jobs to put himself through college." Politicians don't use statistics or research to connect with voters; they use specific, individual examples because when you can attach real stories to ideas, they're going to resonate differently. They're going to be more powerful.

As you go through this list of what worrying might look like, try to identify specific examples of times when you've used these worrying tactics. Don't stop at, *Oh yeah, I definitely do that.* Keep going and try to get more specific. Try to connect with your own personal story. Identify a time when you did it. What was the content of your worry? What did it feel like while you were doing it? Did it come with any consequences? How did you feel when you recognized that your mental energy had been wasted? Have you gotten stuck worrying about that same thing again? It's important for you to really grasp and understand your own experience, as this awareness will be essential later on as we focus more on interventions.

Before we get to the list, a quick disclaimer: these categories are not perfect. You'll likely find some overlap. You may know them by another name. Don't sweat it. These terms can be helpful in understanding what worrying is, but that's just the jumping-off point. You can make up any name that you'd like for these processes. While the labels below can help clarify the different embodiments of worrying, our true purpose is simply in helping you to refine your understanding of your own experience. The categories are a bit porous; they may blur together, but taken as a whole, they paint a picture of the landscape of the worrying processes.

Rumination. This is "figuring it out" on steroids. It's problem-solving gone wild. Like most forms of worrying, rumination is born of a really useful behavior. We all need some analysis in our lives. We have these giant brains and the amazing ability to form complex thoughts. We can hold concepts in our minds—envisioning ideas, mentally representing scenarios, and running through simulations all within our heads. There's not another living species on our planet that can hold a candle to our brain power. But...we can get a little carried away. It's not easy to wield this kind of power. Rumination happens when we forget to set limits. We keep going and going even after we've extracted the useful parts, trying to squeeze more out of the lemon when there's nothing left to squeeze.

Fun fact: the word rumination comes from the Latin *ruminare*, which means to "to chew over again." It originally referred to grazing animals, like cows and sheep, which rechew their food. They eat grass, let it digest and ferment in their stomach, then regurgitate it and chew some more before swallowing it again. Essentially, they throw up in their mouths and then eat it. Gross. Unfortunately, this is what you're doing with your thoughts: regurgitating thoughts to reexamine and extract something useful, long after the utility has faded.

I remember when we bought our first house. It was a big decision and, like many people without a limitless budget, we were forced to make some decisions about what to prioritize. Do we get the house with more kids in the neighborhood? More square footage? Better schools? Bigger yard? Older house with more character, but more things to fix up? Or newer and blander, but with fewer house projects to take on? There was no correct answer. We could make a list of all the pros and cons, but we could go back and forth about that list indefinitely. This one has better schools. But this one has a bigger yard. Kids need good schools. But kids like big yards. But the schools. The yard. The schools. The yard. We could inspect this decision from every angle. Envision every future version of our family. And if we had allowed ourselves to do that, we would never have bought a house. We would have been stuck in analysis paralysis forever. This is what rumination is all about. It's putting the pedal to the floor when you're in neutral. Sifting and churning without taking action.

Rumination tends to be synonymous with worrying, and we'll use them interchangeably throughout this book. Rumination is a way of describing a perseverative thought process. While the other categories below all depict versions of worrying that are a bit more specific, they could probably all fall under the umbrella of rumination as well. Sometimes you'll notice that people refer to rumination as a process specific to past-focused repetitive thoughts, like when you perseverate on a past mistake; you may also hear it used with an emphasis on negative thoughts, as is often the case with depression. Even in the field of psychology, there are varied definitions and applications. We'll use a broader definition in this book that captures the many different iterations of unhelpful thinking, though none of these varied definitions are necessarily correct or incorrect.

Mental review/Mental checking. This is when you conjure up memories of past experiences to try to gain more clarity. Unfortunately, this is like a game of telephone: the more you check and inspect these memories, the less clear they become. Remember, a memory is just a type of thought. A memory about a past event is still just a mental representation. It's subject to bias, perception, and distortion. It degrades over time, infiltrated by over-examination and doubt.

As a general rule of thumb, we tend to have the most useful and constructive reflection immediately after an experience. For example, let's say you go to a job interview and come away saying, *I think that went well. I was a little nervous at first and I probably could have come up with a better answer to that question about my last job, but overall, that was good.* Then you go home and think about it some more. You start to wonder about some of the other things you said. You start to imagine other answers that could have been better. You wonder if your tone was friendly enough? Or maybe it was overly friendly and unprofessional? You don't hear from the employer immediately, and now doubt starts to creep in and you become more critical, picking up minor flaws that are less and less important. You had already gleaned the useful bits right when you walked out of the interview, but by reviewing it over and over again, doubt starts to compromise your memory. In an effort to cull more and more information, you lapse into an incessant examination, checking your memory to see if you can uncover a new tidbit that will provide clarity. What you really want to know is whether or not you got the job, but since you have no ability to think your way to that answer, you'll just keep spinning. Like many aspects of worrying, this process is about striving for certainty, even after it's become apparent that absolute clarity is not an option. If you can't have an answer, you just think a lot instead.

Needing to know/Mental rehearsal. This one is like mental review, but rather than focusing on what has already happened, this process seeks to find clarity in the future. It's running through a thousand scenarios, planning for the improbable events that, however unlikely, can't be ruled out definitively. There's nothing wrong with anticipating cause and effect, assembling what you know about your surroundings to make a guess about what might happen. But this can start to unravel when we keep running mental simulations past the point of diminishing returns.

These types of worrying often start with "what if." *What if my flight is delayed and I miss my connection? What if I make a fool of myself at the party? What if I fail this test? What if I blurt out something offensive? What if I choose the wrong restaurant? What if I'm not cut out for this job? What if I regret my choices?*

We don't get to know the future. We don't get to see which choice will be the best. Once we go through a door, all the other doors are shut. We can't look ahead to see how all of our potential choices will play out and we can't look back to know what would have happened if we'd made a different choice. We just get one shot to make a decision and go for it. This can be pretty maddening. It's a lot of pressure! But remember, the "right" choice is a theoretical idea. To be able to truly assess the best path, you'd need to be able to see every one of these alternate universes—compute each and every infinite option and select the best one. But you can't do that. You're stuck in one universe and get to see only one path that your life will take. You'll have to make do with just making reasonable choices, without ever knowing what could have been. Every choice will always have to be made without knowing how it will all pan out.

Seeking reassurance. This behavior is typically associated with the more tangible version—verbally asking others for reassurance. This is not your average question-asking, which is primarily about gathering information. When you genuinely seek information, you tolerate ambiguity. You allow for incomplete or unsatisfying answers. You ask questions that others are capable of answering. Alternatively, when you're seeking reassurance, you want certainty. In the face of ambiguity, you continue to push, willing yourself to cram the messiness of life into a neatly wrapped package with a bow. You want to be promised, "It's all going to be okay," even though we all know that kind of affirmation is not really possible.

We can sometimes do a mental version of this too. We tell ourselves it will be okay. We repeat that mantra or reassuring thought to find some relief. We attempt to convince ourselves that everything will be fine, rather than acknowledging the hard truth that we simply cannot always be certain.

What's the Function?

By familiarizing yourself with the different manifestations of worrying, the goal is to construct a model of what your worry looks like, but perhaps the most important part of that model is not necessarily *what* worry looks like, but *what for*. Why do you do this? What purpose is it serving?

I like to give people the benefit of the doubt. I try to assume that every behavior, no matter how problematic or ineffective, is useful in some way. It must be achieving something, even if it's not clear at first glance. That kid who's "acting out" is receiving some much-needed attention; the person mired in addiction is getting temporary relief from their emotional pain. Even though these behaviors might not be ideal, they must be working on some level in order for people to keep doing them. In the moments when behaviors seem the most perplexing, people are often prioritizing short-term benefit over long-term gain. They've chosen to relieve acute discomfort, knowing that it might cost them at some point down the road.

The *function* of worrying—what it is doing for you—is an essential piece of the puzzle. This is why I'm less concerned about what particular diagnosis you might have or what label we slap on your brand of worry. Diagnosis is a way of approximating what's going on—looking at the outward symptoms so that you can determine which treatment will be most helpful. It's not bad, per se, but it doesn't tell us exactly what we need to know. Alternatively, looking at the function of your behavior cuts straight to the heart; it asks, "What is this behavior doing for you and what is it that you need to learn so that you won't need to engage in worrying anymore?"

Worrying is complex. It gets woven into your life in nuanced ways, filling different functions and serving multifaceted purposes. Everyone is unique. You'll need to perform your own functional analysis, determining how your worrying serves you specifically. While it's probably a bit simplistic to narrow this analysis down to two factors, there are usually two primary functions that worrying is *intended* to accomplish: find certainty and reduce distress.

Worrying is meant to find certainty. It's incredibly enticing to be able to erase any semblance of doubt; to *know* definitively that you made the right choice. That you weren't irresponsible. That there couldn't have been a better outcome. That you are safe. You want to live a life unencumbered by loose ends and regret. Your awareness of something being incomplete gnaws at you. You want thorough, meticulous, comprehensive. Anything less means there's more work to be done. You want to shine a light on the shadow of doubt, illuminating the best path through life. Sound familiar?

Worry is often the recognition of incompleteness. In a world marred by uncertainty, doubt perpetually swirling around you, a question rises to the surface of your awareness. And in that moment of recognition, you might choose to solve the mystery. You engage in worrying, hoping against hope that you'll finally nail down the unsolvable questions plaguing your life. Uncertainty, or rather, the intolerance of uncertainty, is a common thread running through many aspects of worrying. The quest for a neat and satisfying resolution frequently drives this behavior. It's understandable—it's likely born out of a tireless commitment to do better, driven by a willingness to pursue the important things in your life—but worrying begins to deviate from that path. Despite your good intentions, you get mired in thought rather than called to action.

Some questions you might ask yourself:

- Do you need certainty to be who you want to be?

- Whether you know you're a good person or you're unsure if you're good, would it change who you want to be and how you show up in the world? Can you still try to be who you want to be without knowing?

- Did you actively decide that certainty was important to you? Or did you just find yourself prioritizing it without conscious thought?

Worrying is meant to reduce distress. Worrying is about emotional regulation. Worry feels uncomfortable. Maybe it shows up as anxiety, the initial worry thought setting off a cascade of fears about what might happen. Or it could be guilt, believing that you have a moral or ethical responsibility to ruminate, even when it comes at a cost. Or maybe it's the harder-to-nail-down feeling of incompleteness, the pang of something being not quite right and the inability to feel settled until you close the loop. Whether anxiety, guilt, incompleteness, or something else, these uncomfortable emotional experiences fuel worrying.

The distress that you feel when you encounter uncomfortable emotions propels you to seek relief, to find the solution that makes the uncomfortable feelings go away. Some people turn to drugs or alcohol to subdue their uncomfortable feelings. Others take up exercise or indulge in gambling or sex. Some try to avoid triggers all together. Like these other strategies, worrying acts as a mechanism to reduce distress—it's a form of experiential avoidance, a tool to tamp down the rougher edges of your mind and feel a sense of control over your surroundings. While worrying may provide some temporary relief, it unfortunately comes at a long-term cost.

Some questions to consider:

- What will happen if you live a life dictated by the avoidance of emotions? A life where you only react, but never act? Would that help or harm your efforts to be the person you want to be?

- What are you teaching yourself when you avoid thoughts and feelings? What do you learn about your resilience? About your capacity to do hard things?

Anxiety Is a Responsive System

If worrying is so unhelpful, then why do we still do it? In the next chapter, we're going to explore what makes your worry and anxiety tick. To dismantle anxiety, you first have to understand what keeps it going. You need the instruction manual to deconstruct it and build a more adaptive response. Anxiety can seem complicated—it doesn't always make sense and it can feel like there's no rhyme or reason to its shenanigans—but there are some basic principles that can help you to make sense of your anxiety system and learn how to make it work for you more efficiently.

CHAPTER TWO

What Perpetuates Worry?

That the birds of worry and care fly over your head,
this you cannot change, but that they build nests in
your hair, this you can prevent.

—Chinese Proverb

If you struggle with anxiety, you may be surprised to hear that anxiety is not actually your problem. I know it sure seems like it sometimes, but anxiety itself is not necessarily an issue. At the end of the day, it's an internal experience; a swell of thoughts and feelings. Anxiety becomes problematic when we respond to it in ways that amplify and perpetuate it. So, rather than trying to make anxiety go away, we want to investigate what leads anxiety to become problematic and whether *that* can be changed. We want to ask the questions, *What is going on that is preventing my brain from recognizing that I'm not in danger? Why hasn't my brain corrected the error?*

The Nature of Anxiety

I know we've just met, but I'm going to ask you to get a little uncomfortable. I want to set the stage for how you're going to redefine your relationship with anxiety. You're not going to treat it like it's untouchable or taboo. Anxiety is not the floor in a game of "The Floor is Lava"; it doesn't need to be treated with such reverence. You're going to reclaim it and walk all over it.

Let's try an experiment: Find a quiet place to sit, close your eyes, and for the next minute I want you to try to be anxious. See if you can get that fight or flight system going. See if by just sitting with your eyes closed, you can get your heart rate up, your breathing short.

Go ahead—I'll wait.

Really, it's just a minute. You can do it.

Okay, great. What did you do to try to be anxious? Did you focus on stressors in your life? Did you remind yourself of something scary that's happened to you? Or imagine an embarrassing moment? Or maybe you tried to intentionally dysregulate your breathing. Maybe you believed your anxiety would become out of control and the mere thought of making yourself anxious made you anxious. Or maybe you think that anxiety is dangerous and this whole exercise felt reckless.

Let's try another experiment. This one will be easier—I promise. Sit down again, close your eyes, and this time I want you to try to lift your leg. If you're not able to lift your leg, find another body part to move. Okay, go!

What'd you do this time? Not much, right? In the quick flash of your neurons firing, you told your brain to move your leg and it moved. Pretty simple. Assuming you don't have any physical ailments, it was probably a fairly effortless experience.

Do you see the difference? We have the ability to directly control our bodies; we do not directly control our anxiety. When I told you to try to get anxious, you didn't just flip the anxiety switch in your brain and turn it on. No, instead, you attempted to access anxiety by tinkering with peripheral experiences—thoughts, sensations, and memories. You cannot turn anxiety on and off. It's the byproduct of other processes.

So, we can't manipulate anxiety directly—there is no switch. But you can learn about the processes that affect anxiety so that you can focus your efforts in places where you actually have a hope of having an impact. In this chapter, we'll learn about the processes that perpetuate anxiety and worry so that you can channel your efforts more effectively.

You Need Anxiety

Anxiety is an incredibly useful emotion. It keeps you safe, alerting you to potential threats and preparing you to respond if needed. But like any threat detection system, it works best when it can pick up the *earliest* signs of danger. The smoke detector in your house wouldn't be very useful if it went off only when your house was already burned down. It's meant to catch the smaller indicators of danger to give you a chance to escape or prevent catastrophe, erring on the side of caution so that you can get a jump on the potential threat. If you've ever burnt something on the stove, you've probably noticed that this system is not 100 percent accurate; smoke detectors sometimes pick up on things that are *like* a fire, but that are not actually dangerous. Candles, incense, burnt food, even dust— these things all share characteristics of something dangerous, but they're not necessarily harmful. If your smoke detector is too finely calibrated, you're going to get a lot of false positives.

Your brain's threat detection operates in the same way. It learns about what's dangerous and makes assumptions by finding things that are *like* danger. It prefers to err on the side of caution to keep you safe. This part of your brain is a relic of another time, a time when humans faced more immediate threats, like starvation or predators.

A Sheep Is Not a Bear

Let's imagine that I'm a caveman and I watch my caveman friend get eaten by a black bear. I'd likely conclude that the man-eating bear was dangerous. And rightly so! If I'm a smart caveman, I'll likely run back to my cave to avoid suffering the same fate. But if I'm a *really* smart caveman, I won't stop there. I'll start to make some assumptions: I won't assume that just the man-eating bear was dangerous—I'll assume that *all black bears* are dangerous; or better yet, that *all bears* are dangerous. Black bears, grizzly bears, polar bears, panda bears, koala bears…back to the cave! This is called *generalization*. What would happen if I didn't general- ize? If I saw my friend get eaten, then saw another bear and said, "Well, *this one* is probably a nice bear," I wouldn't last too long. I would have been naturally selected out thousands of years ago.

Your brain's ability to generalize is adaptive. Without it, you'd have to relearn these things over and over again. Since every situation we encounter is unique, we need to be able to pull from similar past situations to make a quick assumption about the current one.

But what happens when you *overgeneralize?* What if I see a black *sheep* and my primitive caveman brain says, *It's fuzzy, black, four legs, snout... quick, back to the cave!* If I respond to this misinterpretation by fleeing, my brain is going to say, *Phew! That was a close one! Good thing you ran; otherwise, you would have been eaten by that bear-ish thing.* It will come to the conclusion that I have narrowly escaped peril, learning that a) sheep are dangerous, and b) I am safe only because I took precautions.

To detect danger—to do its job—sooner, your brain has to make a guess. It connects dots and finds correlations, leaving it up to you to confirm or refute its hypothesis about danger. Your actions in these moments will determine how your brain interprets the potential threats around you. Ultimately, when your brain overgeneralizes, the adaptive part of your threat detection system ceases to be adaptive.

Blame Nicolas Cage

In his book, *Spurious Correlations,* Tyler Vigen (2015) uncovered some unsettling information. For example, did you know that from 1999 to 2009, the number of people who died by drowning in swimming pools correlates with the number of movies that Nicolas Cage appeared in? Or that the rate of divorce in Maine correlates with per capita consumption of margarine? Does this mean we should prosecute Nicolas Cage for his role in these drownings? Or ban margarine in Maine to save marriages? Probably not. Correlation is not causation. Being able to connect the dots is not meaningful in and of itself. Our rational brain is able to use logic and reasoning to make these distinctions, but unfortunately, that part of our brain is not also in charge of our emotional response.

We have the somewhat maddening ability to know rationally that something does not make sense and yet feel anxiety anyway. There are billions of synapses and neural pathways in our brain, but somehow the parts of our brain can't get themselves on the same page when faced with the things that provoke our anxiety. Our high and mighty prefrontal cortex can't be bothered to traffic in such trivial matters; it prefers to leave these things to our amygdala and other "low brain" structures. And if our amygdala had its way, Nicolas Cage would be in a jail cell right now. It's happy to sound the emotional alarm any time it detects something remotely resembling danger. Sadly, our prefrontal cortex won't be much help here. We'll have to find other ways to help our brains make sense of the threats around us.

In the end, if you want to adjust your brain's threat detection system, you have to play the long game: you need to feed your brain information—and not just any information; your brain responds best to *experience*. You'll need to craft experiential opportunities for your brain to learn new information. You'll need to understand how your behavior—your response to anxiety—can either reduce your fear or strengthen it, free you from anxiety or keep you entrenched in it.

Imagine that you're scrolling through your social media account and you see an ad for shoes. If you click on that ad, what are you going to get? More ads for shoes! In fact, just pausing to hover over the ad may be enough to get you more ads for shoes. The algorithm tracks your behavior—what you respond to, what you pay attention to, what you engage with—and learns through each and every interaction. Your brain's the same way; when you dignify an anxiety or worry that comes up, it "serves" you more of what inspired that anxiety and worry—draws more of your attention to it. And now your algorithm isn't working for you. It doesn't necessarily reflect what's important to you or what you're interested in, but what's best at grabbing your attention. If you want this to change, now you've got to figure out how to use the algorithm to your advantage. The algorithm can work for you or against you, and it's up to you to figure out how to make the most of it, say, by scrolling right by the ads for shoes—that is, paying attention to things you want more of and not paying attention to the things keeping you stuck.

If you want your brain's threat detection system to recalibrate, you'll need to be intentional about what information you provide it. Do you respond only to things that are actually dangerous? Or do you get caught paying attention to the false alarms? It's your job to reinforce the accurate indicators of danger while scrolling right by the pretenders—learning to observe them as they arise, *without* immediately acting on them.

To do this, it'll help to know more about the precise cycle of internal experience and behavior that turns worry and anxiety from a momentary blip into a perpetual problem.

Anxiety's Self-Perpetuating Cycle

Underneath the hood of most problems with anxiety, there are three basic components: thoughts, feelings, and behavior. These components form a cycle of reinforcement that drives anxiety and worrying. This feedback loop goes by many names—the anxiety cycle, the OCD cycle, anxiety loops, the vicious cycle of anxiety, and so forth. Whatever you call it, the important takeaway is that we're talking about a self-perpetuating cycle. You can think of it like a fire, which needs oxygen, fuel, and heat to burn. If you deprive it of any of those things, the fire will go out. Anxiety works in a similar way: If you remove the reinforcing behavior, the cycle will peter out on its own. But as long as you keep supplying anxiety with what it needs, you'll continue to have combustion. Here's how the cycle works:

Step 1. Have a thought. Your brain is really good at this. It generates tons of thoughts. Sometimes it notices an external trigger and generates a corresponding thought, and sometimes it can spontaneously come up with thoughts all on its own, without any encouragement. These are often observations about what's happening around you and what might happen in the future. For example, *You might fail that test* or *That person didn't smile at you.* It's your brain's attempt to keep you aware of all the things

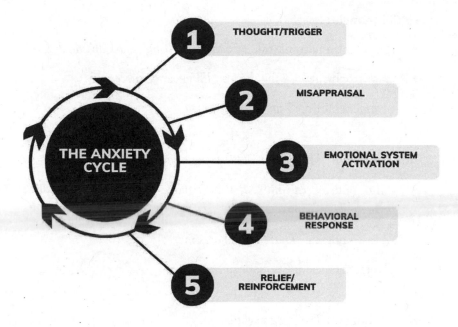

around you, taking in as much raw data as it can. This could also be the awareness of physiological indicators—a pain, a sensation, an urge, and so forth, or an imagined scenario that arises in your awareness, unbidden. Our brains are constantly generating tons and tons of content. Much of it is garbage, unfortunately—spam. But we need to sift through it, nonetheless.

Step 2. Misappraise that thought. Now your brain needs to interpret the raw data. We need to make meaning out of the jumble of cognitions that flood our minds, but we don't always hit the nail on the head. Sometimes our guesses at meaning miss the mark and can become unhelpful. These are called *cognitive distortions*. We often apply formulas or rules to our experiences to make sense of them; unfortunately, some of these rules are littered with biases and misinterpretations—distortions. Below are examples of several common cognitive distortions: all-or-nothing thinking, or a tendency to think in extremes; catastrophizing, or fearing the worst outcome and assuming it will come to pass; and overgeneralizing, or taking one instance as representing all possible instances.

Initial thought: *I might fail.*

- All-or-nothing thinking: *If I can't do it right, I shouldn't do it at all.*

- Catastrophizing: *If I fail the test, I'll never be successful.*

- Overgeneralizing: *I fail at everything.*

Initial thought: *That person didn't smile at me.*

- All-or-nothing thinking: *If I can't make people smile, I shouldn't bother talking to anyone.*

- Catastrophizing: *That person hates me.*

- Overgeneralizing: *Everyone hates me.*

Initial thought: *The stove might be on.*

- All-or-nothing thinking: *If I'm not 100 percent sure, that means I'm negligent and irresponsible.*

- Catastrophizing: *If I'm not sure, the house will burn down.*

- Overgeneralizing: *I shouldn't ever trust myself.*

Initial thought: *I feel tightness in my chest.*

- All-or-nothing thinking: *If everything's not perfect, something is wrong.*

- Catastrophizing: *If I'm feeling tightness in my chest, that must mean I'm having a heart attack.*

- Overgeneralizing: *I'll never feel normal again.*

These misinterpretations mean that the random thoughts that show up in our heads start to take on new meaning, potentially getting flagged in our brains as relevant, meaningful, or worse—dangerous. Which kind of cognitive distortion do you most often experience? Take a second to jot down a few so you have a sense of how your misappraisal may feed the anxiety cycle.

Step 3. Activate emotional system. When your initial thoughts are misappraised, your brain flags them as potentially dangerous and your emotional system becomes activated. You start to get uncomfortable. Your body has been alerted that there *might* be danger, so it starts to prepare.

This step has two important parts. You're probably pretty familiar with the first part—your body starts preparing for potential danger physiologically, which you might experience as shortness of breath, tightness in your chest, increased heart rate, sweating, gastrointestinal distress, and so forth. All those things that make you feel really physically uncomfortable.

But it's actually the second part that's the key to the anxiety cycle. Once your emotional system is activated, it's now open to receiving new information. Remember, the activation of this system simply means that there *might* be danger, so your brain is now scanning to confirm or refute that hypothesis. It's watching you closely, seeing how you respond, and trying to determine whether it needs to keep this system activated or shut it down.

Step 4. Respond. At this point in the cycle, you're already uncomfortable. I'm going to go out on a limb and guess that you probably don't *like* feeling uncomfortable. You're going to be motivated to find a way to make that feeling go away. Totally understandable. You want relief. Who can blame you?

But remember what we discussed in step 3: once your brain has activated the emotional system and gone on high alert, it's now seeking any potential indicator that there might indeed be danger. If, in that moment, you scramble to make it go away or immediately pivot into problem-solving mode, your brain gets confirmation that there *was* a problem! It learns that it was correct to have set off that system. After all, if there were no danger, why would you jump into action? And the next time you encounter this type of situation, your brain will once again assume that it's dangerous.

Many people imagine that the path to an anxiety-free existence is to somehow navigate their way through life without catastrophe. If you can find a way to smooth over the bumps and have everything work out, your brain will finally settle and let its guard down. But it's not just about the end result; it's about how you got there. Let's say, for example, that I touch a doorknob and have the thought, *Oh no! What if I get sick?!* If I then wash my hands (and presumably, don't get sick), all that my brain has learned is that I am safe *because* I washed my hands. If I had not washed them? Certain doom. It's tempting to think that as long as everything works out, our brains will adjust. But as long as there are conditions attached—like washing your hands after you touch a doorknob that feels contaminated, which might save you from getting sick or might do nothing at all—you don't have any way of knowing for sure. Your brain assumes that these qualifiers are meaningfully related to the outcome. As far as it's concerned, you're safe not because danger never existed; you're safe because of the actions you took to prevent danger.

Sadly, this is a pretty unfair test for your brain to put you through. Your brain is essentially saying, "If you respond like there's danger, I'll assume there is danger; if you respond like everything is fine, I'll assume that everything is fine." Except the trick is, you have to pass this test while *feeling* like there's danger. The activation of your emotional system is happening at the exact same time that you have to take this test! You're already feeling the physiological aspects of danger, so of course you're going to want to try to make that feeling go away. Anxiety has its thumb on the scale, pushing you toward an unnecessary response.

Step 5. Receive short-term relief and reinforcement. Anxiety sucks. It's really uncomfortable. You want it to just go away. And so, perhaps against your better judgment, you give in and do something to get temporary relief. You probably suspect that everything will be fine (your rational brain tells you so), but just to play it safe, you err on the side of caution and find something to make it all feel better. This could be an overt, external behavior designed to mitigate risk, or it could be a mental process, such as trying to gain certainty that everything will be okay.

Whatever action you choose, you are rewarded with a temporary reprieve from distress.

When you make your discomfort go away, it's called *negative reinforcement*. Reinforcers are things that either incentivize or disincentivize a behavior; that is, they make it more likely or less likely that a behavior will happen again. There are four types of behavioral reinforcement that you can leverage—two of which, negative and positive reinforcement, result in more of a behavior, and two of which, punishment and extinction, result in less. Negative reinforcement powers the anxiety cycle. When you perform a compulsion or engage in worrying, you temporarily buy yourself short-term relief, but in doing so, you've now strengthened the behavior. *Positive reinforcement* is when a behavior results in a positive reward. *Punishment* is when a behavior results in an adverse consequence that compels you to do less of the behavior, and *extinction* is when a positive reward is removed.

Here's an example: I take my child to the grocery store, and when we're going through the check-out aisle, he asks for a candy bar. I say no, but he whines and then I give in and buy him a candy bar. In doing this, I have *positively reinforced* this behavior for my son—he gets a reward for his whining behavior. At the same time, I am also *negatively reinforcing* my own behavior—the discomfort of having a whining kid at the grocery store has now been temporarily removed. We'll both be more likely to resort to these behaviors again in the future, since the behaviors had their intended effect.

If, at some point, I end up with a kid who has a mouthful of cavities or who whines to get his way all the time, I may want to try to change this behavior. This time, when we go through the checkout aisle, he whines, but I stand firm with my no, and his behavior will now be put on *extinction*—the behavior is no longer resulting in the positive reward. He'll be less likely to attempt this behavior again, since it did not have the intended effect. Alternatively, I could impose consequences for my kid, which would be *punishment*.

When it comes to anxiety, short-term relief comes with a steep trade-off. Each time you behave in ways that might give you short-term relief, you're strengthening that association, reinforcing your brain's interpretation of danger, and whittling away at your ability to tolerate distress and uncertainty. In this regard, you can think of it almost like addiction: you may indeed get some immediate relief, but you're going to need more and more over time, and you won't learn that you don't need a substance to manage the ups and downs of life. Anxiety, like all painful emotional experiences, is uncomfortable, but not dangerous and not permanent. If you wait it out, like a kid crying at the checkout aisle, it will eventually settle and subside.

This Is Counterintuitive

Everyone wants to make their distress go away. Our brains have been programmed through thousands of years of evolution to set off this emotional system and we, as human beings, have survived because we've paid attention to that alarm. But evolution works slowly. Our current brains are optimized for humans who existed thousands of years ago. We're no longer in constant danger from predators or famine. Maybe in another hundred thousand years or so, humans will have developed brains that are equipped to navigate our modern world. And unfortunately, it will be of little use to them, just like our brains are a bit obsolete for us. Such is life. The imperfect lag time of evolution is something we'll just have to accept.

So cut yourself some slack. Your response is not a bad one. It makes a lot of sense. But if you can learn to allow anxiety to exist without trying to make it go away, without perpetuating the anxiety cycle, you'll be short-circuiting thousands of years of evolution. That's no small task. It's counterintuitive and it's going to take some practice, but it can be done.

The next chapter will discuss the controllability of anxiety and worrying, giving you a blueprint for how to dismantle a habit which seems to have taken root.

CHAPTER THREE

Can Worry Be Controlled?

Have no fear of perfection—you'll never reach it.

—Salvador Dalí

Clients frequently tell me that they believe their anxiety cannot be changed, that their minds can't possibly work any other way. The way things are is the way things are and any effort to change that would be an exercise in futility. They were born anxious and this is simply how it will always be.

As you might imagine, I'm not a huge fan of this idea—I suppose I wouldn't make a very good therapist if I thought that change was a hopeless endeavor. Of course, you may have never known another way of being in the world—and if so, I can't blame you for feeling this way either. If all you've ever known is worry, then that's what you'll come to expect. But this outlook strips you of any agency to grow and learn new ways to interact with the world. The habit of worrying is not inevitable. In this chapter, we'll explore the places where you may indeed face limitations, but we'll also delve into where you have potential for changing your worrying habit.

Top Five Reasons You Can't Change

To start, I'm going to share with you some of the common rationales that my clients cite when they characterize this anxious way of being as an inevitability. Each one of these reasons is true…but incomplete. They're missing some important context. You may want to grab a notebook (or be prepared to scribble in the margins). Each of the following rationales will include a brief writing exercise so that you can begin challenging some of your assumptions about worrying.

1. I'm genetically prone to anxiety.

Sure, this is probably accurate. I'm not familiar with your specific gene pool, but evidence does suggest that genetics play a role in anxiety. Some people come packaged with a more robust emotional system. This could mean that you experience emotions more intensely—you feel deeply, or your emotions go from zero to sixty quickly and take a while to come back down again. It may mean that you're more susceptible to behavioral reinforcement mechanisms—that is, some folks can get away with occasional undesirable behaviors without their actions snowballing into habits; however, you might get trapped in your habits almost immediately, with little margin for error. It could mean that you're more liable to become immersed in imagination, feeling the simulated scenarios in your head as if they were real. Or maybe you're highly attuned to the physiological aspects of anxiety, noticing each subtle change in heart rate and inadvertently activating that fear system in your brain out of an abundance of caution. Ultimately, whatever your flavor of anxiety, these things do generally have some basis in genetics.

So, it's safe to say that in the battle of nature versus nurture, nature does indeed have a role to play. But so does nurture. The experiences you've had—the life events, the upbringing, the messages and beliefs that you've absorbed throughout your life—these things all play a part in determining how you relate to anxiety. So will your behaviors and the ways you choose to respond to anxiety now. To boil it all down to a genetically predetermined fate is unfair and incomplete.

It's also important to note that anxiety disorders are not permanent. The mechanisms that drive a struggle with anxiety may be innate tendencies, but you can learn how to manage those tendencies. There are plenty of people who seek treatment and improve to the point that they no longer meet diagnostic criteria for an anxiety disorder. Their DNA hasn't changed. Their genes are still their genes. But they've learned to pour their energy into the aspects of this problem that *are* in their control. They can create new experiences, reform their beliefs, and develop skills to respond and relate to anxiety more effectively. The genetic component will always be what it is, but it's important to remember that genes are just one piece of the puzzle and you can get good results without ever changing that part of the equation. To focus on the one part that's outside of your control is not very helpful.

The "disorder" in anxiety disorder implies that these symptoms interfere with your functioning; they get in the way. Anxiety is inescapable—we all feel it, we all *need* to feel it—that does not mean that it needs to get in the way. By learning to relate differently to your distress, you can minimize the impact that it has on your life. The presence of anxiety does not need to be synonymous with impairment.

Try This for Yourself. What other genetic predispositions do you have? Are you naturally athletic or do you have two left feet? Are you introverted or extroverted? How have you adjusted or changed your life to play to your strengths and adjust for the places where you struggle? Jot down some notes about how you've been able to manage or build other skills that may not have come naturally.

2. But I have an anxiety disorder!

Labels can be useful. They allow you to understand your experience better, feel less alone, and connect with others with similar experiences. They can even help to inform which type of treatment might be the most helpful. But they also come with some drawbacks.

When you allow this label to become the center of your identity, you start to build a narrative around it. This is who you are. This is how you'll always be. It becomes a character trait rather than a current snapshot of your experience. You're currently struggling to manage anxiety in an effective way, but that doesn't necessarily mean it will always be that way.

In her book *Mindset* (2007), Carol Dweck, a psychologist studying motivation, described the difference between a "growth mindset" and a "fixed mindset." Those with a fixed mindset believe that their intelligence, skills, and abilities are stable, unchanging character traits. You are who you are. If you have a fixed mindset, failure becomes a direct reflection of you and your innate abilities. So, you're less likely to challenge yourself or take risks. Those with a growth mindset, on the other hand, believe that they have the capacity to change—that through their efforts they can build and improve their skills. If you have a growth mindset, you're much more likely to seek out a challenge, as it represents an opportunity to learn. You know that failure or mistakes are not indictments of your character, but instead merely indicate that you have an opportunity to grow.

Interestingly, these ideas have nothing to do with your natural starting point (and actually, it doesn't matter what deficits may exist or where your organic starting line is). They're simply an observation that if you approach things in one way, you'll improve, and if you approach them in another, you won't. If I say, "I suck at math," and believe that to be an irrefutable, permanent state of being, I'm probably not going to put much time into studying for that math test. After all, it's a foregone conclusion that I'm going to fail. If instead I say, "Math is hard for me right now, but by studying and putting time into math, I can get better," I'll have a reason to try and will be more likely to improve. If we believe that we don't have the capacity to change, we're not going to be very invested in change. And this is true, irrespective of our innate starting point. Whether or not I truly suck at math is not relevant; what's important is that whatever my current skill level, I can improve it by putting in work.

Does your anxiety make things more difficult? Of course! But you have the capacity to get better at the skills required to manage that anxiety. You can be someone with anxiety who has built skills to manage it or someone with anxiety who hasn't. It's up to you.

Like many things in this book, practicing a growth mindset is exactly that—a practice. It's not something you'll magically have once you simply decide to adopt it; you must actively notice moments when you've become stuck in a fixed mindset and give yourself a prompt to shift your perspective. You can think of it sort of like mindfulness—you don't just decide to be mindful and—poof!—now you're officially mindful forevermore. It's an ongoing, continuous effort that will require active, in-the-moment awareness. But if you can put in the effort to practice, it'll become easier and easier to do, and in time you'll experience real rewards.

Try This for Yourself. Try writing down some of those "fixed mindset" thoughts. While they can show up anywhere, see if you can identify some of the repeat offenders—those stories you've told yourself a million times before. Where do you find yourself feeling stuck or hopeless? Next, see if you can apply a "growth mindset" lens to those thoughts. What skills could you acquire or practice to help you grow?

3. I'll never be worry free.

That's probably true. You have very little hope of stumbling into a life without any stressors, without anything that evokes concern. You'll probably have your share of things that cause you to feel worried or anxious. In some ways, that's probably a good thing. To not have worry is to have nothing to lose. And I hope you have lots to lose. I hope you have meaning and purpose, people you care about, an investment in your future. We can't have things that matter without simultaneously being aware that they could all evaporate. To be alive is to be aware that we could lose it all.

Remember, the goal of this book is not to make you worry free. That kind of all-or-nothing thinking is unhelpful, as it creates an impossible goal, setting you up for failure. But let's not let this absence of complete bliss get in the way of something that could still be pretty great. Life is rarely one extreme or the other, but rather something in the middle. You may have moments where the awareness of pain is uncomfortable, where your vision of the perfect outcome is shattered by the imperfect reality. But you don't need to be assured of unparalleled success in order to take a step toward your goal. For instance, I know I'll never play basketball like Michael Jordan. In the abstract, I suppose anything's possible, but I'm starting to suspect that, as a not-especially-athletic five-foot-seven middle-aged man, my chances are starting to fade. But that doesn't mean I can't get better at basketball. I don't need to measure myself against the pinnacle of possibility, but instead, I can focus on where I am now and how I can build on that. Does that take me to the NBA? I suspect not. But does it improve my current situation and make me feel more accomplished and more fulfilled? Absolutely.

Try This for Yourself. Being worry free is an all-or-nothing, perfectionistic approach to worry that tends to get in the way. It's hard to find a one-size-fits-all approach to anything in life. Our personality traits, our preferred methods for doing things—these can be helpful in some places and less helpful in others. For example, impulsivity might be destructive if it results in recklessness or irresponsible spending, but it might come in handy when you're trying to be adventurous or to inject some spontaneity into your life.

With this in mind, consider the perfectionistic approach that you've been using—how is it working for you? Are there places where it works well? Are there places where it gets in your way? How is it working in the context of worrying?

4. My worrying is automatic.

Sometimes the mental process of worrying is intentional. You see exactly what you're doing and choose to do it anyway. But sometimes, it does happen automatically. You're not completely conscious of beginning to worry and find yourself sometime later, having already spent hours lost in your head. If this happens to you, then worrying has become a habit or default setting—the outcome that will happen if we do nothing to interrupt it.

When I put on my pants each day, I put my leg in the left pant leg first. I don't think about this or do it intentionally. I've been dressing myself for a long time and it requires very little mental energy. My brain has bigger fish to fry and for simple tasks it can be on autopilot. So, left pant leg first. Rinse, wash, repeat. But does that mean that I can't ever put my *right* pant leg on first? No! It'd require some effort. I'd have to be much more intentional. I might need to put some sticky notes on the dresser, or cram some old T-shirts into the left pant leg to jog my memory. But it could be done. And I'd wager that if I was consistent enough, I could even get to the point where my right leg became the new default setting.

Such is the case with worrying. You've been doing it for a while and this is what comes naturally at this point. But you're flexible. You can learn new things, build new habits. It will take time, effort, and repetition, but you can always train yourself to become more aware of what you're doing and to start practicing new ways of responding. You have the capacity for change. Simply because you currently engage in a behavior automatically does not mean you can't create change by becoming more intentional. Automatic is not the same as inevitable.

Try This for Yourself. You can't change a habit without being aware of it first. Try keeping a Worry Log. You can use a piece of paper or download a blank copy of this exercise at the publisher's website for this book: http://www.newharbinger.com/52144. Imagine you're a researcher trying to get a snapshot of what your worrying looks like—like Jane Goodall observing the chimps—and keep a record of when you worry. For each instance of worrying, you'll want to write down some relevant details:

- Was there a particular trigger?

- What made this particular thought or trigger so compelling?

- How long did you spend worrying?

- How did you eventually stop?

- What emotions were you feeling before, during, and after worrying?

- Where were you physically (in your car, on the couch, etc.)?

- What was the circumstance? Were you alone or with people? Tired? Hungry? Bored?

You don't need keep the log forever, but you should do it long enough that you think you have a representative sample. You want it to feel like it fairly and accurately depicts what your worry typically looks like. When you're done, take a look and see if you notice any trends. Do any patterns stand out? As you continue to experiment with exercises throughout this book, you may want to look back at this log. It's hard to root out all your worry at once and you may find that it helps to try the approaches in this book in one specific circumstance before attempting to generalize further. For example, when you read about defusion exercises in chapter 9—exercises to begin breaking the habit of becoming *fused* with your own worry thoughts—you may find that it's easier to start by trying to use defusion only when you worry while taking a shower. These interventions require a lot of intentionality and it's really difficult to keep that up all day. Your log can be a way to chop this effort down to size by identifying the circumstances where an intervention would be most useful.

5. I can't stop.

Even this one has a kernel of truth: you *can* stop, but you can't "*just stop.*" We've all had moments where we've looked at that person struggling with behavioral control and wondered, *Why don't they just stop?* Maybe it was the person battling substance abuse or a gambling addiction. Maybe it was the person in the depths of their eating disorder whom we wanted to "just eat." Or the person struggling with hair pulling or skin picking and we couldn't fathom why they wouldn't "just stop." These behaviors can seem so simple. It's tempting to believe that if you want it enough, if you can just summon enough willpower, you'll be able to push through and manifest the life that you want for yourself. But here's the truth: willpower is overrated.

First, often when we feel that we "can't" stop, we're really saying that stopping is hard and complicated and will require more than a quick burst of inspiration. In *The Willpower Instinct*, Kelly McGonigal (2013) proposes a distinction between "will-power" and "won't-power." Will-power refers to the ability to push ourselves through difficult tasks or emotions—the determination to do hard things. Won't-power is more about resistance; it's about inhibiting urges and tamping down impulsivity. When you're refraining from worrying or foregoing the pull the figure it all out, you're likely using won't-power.

Second, the truth is that willpower is a finite resource and it's always in flux. It comes and it goes. One study (Baumeister, Vohs, and Tice 2007) showed that one initial act of self-control impaired subsequent self-regulatory behaviors—in other words, when we rely solely on willpower to get things done, we will deplete our reserves. Brute-force resistance and perseverance may both be necessary sometimes, but we don't want to overly rely on them; and they'll work best when complemented by other motivators.

Try This for Yourself. Every time you've worried, you've eventually stopped worrying. You've forgotten about it, you've fallen asleep, or you've directed your focus to something else. However you've done it, you've somehow managed to end each and every discrete episode of worrying. Aside from willpower, what are some other tools that you can employ to help you discontinue worrying? If it's not about trying harder, what would it look like to try smarter? What skills would you need to master? What concepts would you need to embrace?

The Solution Is Swiss Cheese

If you want to break your habit of worrying, you'll need to concede that wanting isn't enough. The desire to change the habit of worry has to be accompanied by actions that will help you translate that desire into reality. You'll need to approach it from multiple angles. When I treat body-focused repetitive behaviors (hair pulling, skin picking, etc.), one of the most common experiences that I hear about from clients at their initial assessment is, "So I tried using a fidget toy to keep my hands busy, but it didn't work." My response is usually something reasonably compassionate, but my thought is, *Of course it didn't! It's not that simple!* There's nothing wrong with using tools to keep your hands occupied, but that's just one intervention; it only targets one aspect of this behavior. If you want to change this habit, you'll need to tailor interventions to target all the different aspects. You'll need reminders (on your mirror, your phone, the drawer where you keep your tweezers), you'll need accountability (set goals, be around other people, let them know how to support you), you'll need to build adaptive responses to permission-giving thoughts (*Will it really just be this one time? Will you actually stop when you intend to?*), you'll need to identify the situations when you're most vulnerable (evening, car, morning routine, etc.) and the feelings and sensations driving it (boredom, exhaustion, anxiety, asymmetry, incompleteness, etc.). This list is not comprehensive, but you get the idea: you can't just try to stop the symptoms—you have to directly target the mechanisms driving them.

During the coronavirus pandemic, epidemiologists popularized an idea called the "Swiss Cheese Model." The concept is that no intervention is perfect and any single layer of protection will have some holes, but if you stack up enough layers—if you combine things like masks, vaccines, social distancing, hygiene, air filtration, and spending time outdoors rather than indoors—you can eventually achieve sufficiency. Approaching the habit of worrying works in the same way: any single intervention will likely be insufficient, but if you develop a set of skills and target the mechanisms driving your worrying, you'll be able to achieve a more robust effect. Worrying is not just habit, or just getting lost in what-ifs, or *just* anything. It's a complex behavior, necessitating a complex response.

I know that can feel daunting. How can you possibly upend all these longstanding habits? But remember: You don't need to do it perfectly. It doesn't have to be for the noblest of reasons, and it doesn't have to be all in one fell swoop. You just have to make small, incremental changes and stick to them, and they'll add up over time. Think of it like changing the course of an airplane. If you change your course by even a tiny degree, you'll end up in a completely different place if you go far enough. These small changes compound and grow, but you have to start somewhere.

I usually keep a to-do list on my desk. It helps me to organize and prioritize my thoughts and I create a new one at the beginning of each week. My to-do list has one firm rule: if I don't complete a task by the end of the week, it can't go back on the list in the same way—I have to find some way to break that task down further. Often, I deconstruct the task by identifying the component parts and figuring out which manageable component it'd be best to start with; in that way, I'm able to turn something complex and daunting into something simple and manageable.

In the end, the only way to get stuck in place is to do nothing; as long as you're doing something, you'll be moving forward. And you'll be surprised by how much you can do when you give yourself permission to do it imperfectly.

Coming Up Next...

The next section will focus on changing your relationship to worry. There are ways that you have integrated worry into your life—using it to solve problems or to ensure that you're true to your values—that have not worked as planned. There are ways that you've come to experience your own mind—becoming absorbed in imagined catastrophe or hijacked by the scary content of your thoughts—that have unintentionally strengthened your worry habit. The goal of the next section is to help you to reclaim your mind and these processes so that you can develop new ways of relating to your internal experiences.

PART II

Changing Your Relationship to Worry

CHAPTER FOUR

Focusing on Process,
Not Content

*Don't tell us what to believe, what to fear. Show
us belief's wide skirt and the stitch that unravels
fear's caul.*

—Toni Morrison, "Nobel Lecture"

When you've been relentlessly tormented by the same worries or obsessions for long enough, it can be easy to focus on the content of those thoughts. It can seem like you have a problem with germs or finances or safety or whatever the *worry du jour* happens to be. But that theme is not really your problem. The content is just the bait. It's a trap that lures you in, inadvertently powering the anxiety cycle. You get stuck trying to solve a problem, never realizing that you've been sent on a fool's errand. It's a game of mental whack-a-mole. Turns out, you're the lucky recipient of a lifetime supply of worries! Resolve one, you get another! You'll chase that resolution forever, getting no closer to a worry-free life with a neatly tied bow.

If you want a more adaptive relationship with your internal experiences, you'll need to disentangle yourself from the scary *content* of your thoughts and instead focus on the *nature* of the thoughts. When you can recognize unhelpful patterns of thinking, the content starts to become irrelevant.

You're Special, but Your Content Isn't

You've already learned that there are many different factors contributing to anxiety and worry, but the content of your thoughts does not need to be one of them. In a classic study, Rachman and de Silva (1978) found that intrusive thoughts experienced by people with OCD differed in frequency, duration, intensity, and consequence as compared to folks without OCD. The one thing that was not significantly different? You guessed it—the content of the thoughts! Everybody has intrusive thoughts about the same scary, messed-up stuff, regardless of whether they have OCD. Another study (Wells and Carter 2001) found that folks with GAD don't actually worry about different things than folks without GAD. The difference is that folks with GAD have more negative thoughts and beliefs *about* worry. In other words, they worry about worry! The evidence is clear—the specific thoughts and concerns that you have are not the problem; it's how you relate to them that really matters.

Cognitive Versus Metacognitive Approaches

In traditional cognitive therapy, the main focus is on identifying cognitive distortions in your thinking. Once you've identified an error in your thought process, you can "reframe" that thought in a new, more balanced way. For example, if you have the thought, *I never do anything right*, you may notice that you're employing a distortion called "discounting the positive." You could reframe this thought as, *Even though I made a mistake, I know that there are many times when I am able to complete tasks without any errors*. This reframing of the thoughts allows for a more objective appraisal.

While this strategy can be helpful at times, it does have some pitfalls:

- This exercise can get mixed up in the anxiety cycle. When it's used to provide reassurance or to reduce anxiety, it can inadvertently perpetuate anxiety. Rather than learning to tolerate uncertainty, you may be learning that you need an answer; rather than learning that you can tolerate distress, you may be learning that you need a strategy to escape it.

- This approach can sometimes break down when you're faced with more realistic concerns. If you've just had a heart attack and are experiencing worry about your upcoming bypass surgery, the reframe of "I may die, but I haven't died yet" might fall a bit flat. If you declared bankruptcy recently and you're feeling worry about paying your bills, the reframe of "I may not have any money, but at least I don't have as much debt as I used to" may not do much to allay your very real financial concerns.

- There is an inherent assumption that worry will be eliminated by restoring logic and objectivity. Many people struggling with worry and anxiety are perfectly aware that their concerns are unrealistic or unlikely. The mere possibility, however improbable, is often enough to keep worry going.

- And last, this approach is mired in content! It approaches worry as if the content of these thoughts is the problem, rather than the process.

A metacognitive approach, by contrast, looks at your relationship to thoughts. It sidesteps content all together and instead looks at your thoughts and beliefs *about* anxiety, seeking to examine what it is about your approach to worry that may be keeping you stuck.

Metacognitive Awareness

Everyone feels distressing emotions. Our lives will always contain some ups and downs, moments of joy coupled with moments of pain. The uncomfortable emotions (anger, sadness, anxiety, shame, etc.) are all part of the human experience. It's tempting to idealize a rose-tinted version of our emotional landscape—one that's populated solely by our joyful emotions and our pleasant thoughts. How nice would it be to have a life spared from pain and sadness? Free from intrusive, unwanted thoughts? It's a pretty picture, but I'm sorry to say, you're going to want to come back down to earth and recognize a more realistic ideal. Life involves pain, but it doesn't need to involve suffering.

When you resist and struggle with your unwanted emotions, you only make it worse. Let's say, for example, that you're feeling sad, but you don't want to be sad. That seems reasonable. But then you start to get mad about your inability to extinguish that sadness.

Now, you have sadness + anger.

And let's say maybe you recognize what you just did—you added hardship to hardship—and now you wish you had been more accepting of that initial sadness, so you're feeling a bit guilty about your response.

Now, you have sadness + anger + guilt.

And then, you recognize how unhelpful *that* response was and feel frustrated that you weren't more compassionate with yourself.

Now, you're up to sadness + anger + guilt + anger.

Yikes! You get the idea. This snowballing of emotional responses can get big and unwieldy. Most of us can manage one feeling or another; it's when we start piling them up and compounding them that we get into trouble. The inevitable pain we feel in life starts to grow and multiply until it's become suffering and misery.

The best-case scenario is that unwanted thoughts and feelings plop down into our present moment, and rather than struggling with them, we let them be. We open ourselves up to the experience, whatever it happens to be, and allow it to come and go, deftly navigating the flow of thoughts and feelings. In doing this, we ensure that we don't exacerbate the situation by trying to resist, control, or push it away. In other words, we intentionally respond in a way that clears the path for the feelings to naturally resolve. So that ideal, pain-free existence? Let go of it. The ideal you want to shoot for is one in which you notice your thoughts and feelings and strive to *respond* in a way that doesn't exacerbate the situation. Don't try to control the rain—invest in a good umbrella. Our goal isn't to make uncomfortable feelings go away; rather, it's to notice these feelings and determine what kind of response might be useful.

This requires metacognitive awareness—the ability to step back and observe your experience. It's not just having a thought, but knowing that you're having a thought. You need this additional layer of awareness to make executive decisions about how to proceed. Without it, you're at the mercy of your thoughts, along for the ride wherever your mind takes you. Instead, you can use metacognitive awareness to become more intentional and strategic in your response to anxiety. Once you can step back and see the process unfolding, you can determine what kind of approach will be most helpful.

Metacognitive Beliefs

In metacognitive therapy (MCT), the basic assumption is that dysfunction and psychological disorders can be attributed to a *style* of relating to our emotional experiences that interferes with adaptive learning. Instead of moving toward a resolution of uncomfortable feelings, we get stuck. We relate to the thoughts and feelings in unhelpful ways, maintaining the painful experiences rather than fostering their resolution. Essentially, we clog up the emotional assembly line when we respond in inefficient ways.

This style, as described in MCT, consists of five different domains of metacognitive traits, which have been found to predict proneness to worry, anxiety, and obsessional symptoms (Cartwright-Hatton and Wells 1997). The five categories are positive beliefs, negative beliefs, cognitive confidence, beliefs about the need to control thoughts, and cognitive self-consciousness. In this chapter, we're going to examine this unhelpful style of responding and identify strategies to create a more helpful approach.

Positive Beliefs

This one sounds good, right? It's not often that you'll find a therapist who will deduct points for positive thinking. Well, positive thinking about worrying may be the exception. The belief that worrying is helpful or useful is a very common perspective for folks who may be struggling with anxiety. I often hear things like:

- If I worry, I'll be more prepared.

- Worrying helps me feel in control.

- Worrying allows me to anticipate all the possible outcomes.

- I need to worry to be okay.

- Worrying is how I cope.

Positive beliefs tend not to be too problematic on their own (Wells 2011), but when combined with some other beliefs about worry, they can become part of the problem. Holding on to positive beliefs can tacitly provide permission to continue engaging in worrying and disincentivize you from making a change. While the strategy of worrying may not be entirely bad, it has become problematic for *you*. Think about it as you might conceptualize alcohol for an alcoholic: it may have some positives (it can be fun, disinhibiting, a social activity, etc.), but for the person struggling with alcoholism, it's just not working.

Challenging positive beliefs. It can help to review how effective this strategy has been for you. Often, it's not that the positive belief is *wrong*, it's just that it misses the bigger picture. For example, with the belief "If I worry, I'll be more prepared," we might start to ask questions like:

- Are there other ways for you to be prepared that don't involve worrying?

- If worrying makes you anxious, does that get in the way of your preparation?

- Is there any evidence that worry has actually led to better outcomes?

- Does the fact that things worked out necessarily mean that worrying caused that result?

You could also try using some examples from your life to compare your worries with the reality of what actually happened. Chances are good that you "problem-solved" a thousand possibilities that never came to fruition. The recognition of this inefficiency can help in dismantling the myth that worrying is an effective strategy.

For example, if you worried about an upcoming doctor's appointment, it might look like this:

- *I could get lost on the way to the doctor.*

- *I might miss my appointment.*

- *I hope I don't forget my insurance card and end up with medical debt.*

- *The doctor could think I'm really sick and order a diagnostic test.*

- *What if I need to get a second opinion?*

- *The doctor might completely miss what's wrong and I'll have missed my chance at an early intervention.*

- *I might have to advocate for what I need from the doctor if they're not listening to me.*

- *I might have to find a new doctor.*

The reality that you experienced might have looked more like this:

I went to the doctor, got a checkup, and everything was okay.

Worrying misses the mark quite a bit—there are a lot of false leads. Are there any other strategies in your life that you would keep using with this low of a success rate? If your dog pees outside one out of a hundred times, would you conclude that you had a successful house-training strategy? I suspect not.

Negative Beliefs

This category of beliefs generally involves pessimistic or catastrophized predictions about the consequence of worry. I usually hear things like:

- If I worry, I won't be able to stop.

- I won't be able to handle being anxious.

- I can't control my worrying.

- Worrying is dangerous for my heart and health.

Can you imagine how these kinds of beliefs might impact the experience of worry? How might they change your response? If we believe that worry is perilous or uncontrollable, we'll be much more likely to resort to mitigation strategies, unintentionally responding in ways that maintain and exacerbate worry. We'll assess worry as being more dangerous and we'll also be less invested in strategies to effectively manage worry if we deem it uncontrollable (Bailey and Wells 2015).

Challenging negative beliefs. It can be helpful to gather evidence about these beliefs. It's important to strive to be open to new explanations and curious about gathering more information that may better inform your beliefs or even change your opinions. An open mind allows us to make better sense of the world around us. Let's look at some of the negative beliefs above and see if we can find additional perspectives that might help us come to a more accurate conclusion about the nature of worry:

- *If I worry, I won't be able to stop.* If this were true, it would mean that you are worried 100 percent of the time. What happens to your worry when you sleep? When you get distracted and catch yourself immersed in an activity? No, even for you, worry comes and goes. It's not a constant and it does indeed stop.

- *I won't be able to handle being anxious.* Every time you've been anxious, that anxiety has come and gone. It's had a beginning, middle, and end. You've moved through it and survived each and every time. Throughout your entire life, every time that anxiety has come for you, you've been able to handle it. The current score is Anxiety 0, You 7,826,027. You may not have liked it, but you certainly handled it. In fact, you're probably pretty skilled at being anxious by now.

- *I can't control my worrying.* You can't control your worry, but you can control your worrying. Worrying may be a habit for you, but habits can be changed. It takes time and practice, but you absolutely can learn the skills to manage your worrying.

- *Worrying is dangerous for my heart.* Not exactly. It feels that way sometimes, but people very frequently misinterpret the physiological signs of anxiety and panic, believing that they're in danger. You're increased heart rate? No different than moderate exercise. That feeling like you can't get enough oxygen? That's actually your body getting *too much* oxygen from rapid breathing. Unless you have a serious pre-existing condition, the physiological aspects of worry and anxiety are not acutely dangerous. Anxiety is, however, correlated with some long-term health risks. This means that anxiety doesn't pose much of a threat in the moment, but leaving your anxiety untreated may increase your chances of adverse health effects in the long term (Olafiranye et al. 2011).

Cognitive Confidence

One of the great ironies of worrying is that, despite the intention of finding clarity or certainty, worriers often find themselves less sure. After turning over endless options and scenarios, their mental grasp of the situation becomes muddier. Worrying often has the unfortunate side effect of whittling away at our ability to trust ourselves. When someone with OCD checks a stove, they may initially be checking to see if the stove is off, but the second check? The third check? The tenth check? Now they're checking *themselves*.

- *Am I remembering correctly?*

- *Did I see what I thought I saw?*

- *When I checked, did I mistakenly turn it on when I touched the knob?*

- *Maybe I was distracted when I was checking and now I need to do it again.*

And this isn't just about OCD. This doubt about memory and attention can show up in any number of worries:

- *Can I trust my judgment?*

- *Did I perceive the situation correctly?*

- *Is my inability to focus putting me at risk?*

- *If I can't remember with absolute clarity, that must mean I can't be trusted.*

This category always reminds me of the concept of the "unreliable narrator"—those books and stories where the perception or trustworthiness of the narrator is in question. You don't know whether to believe what you're being told. You spend the entire book questioning, trying to figure out what's going on, unsure if the lens that you're seeing the world through is accurate. By doubting and questioning everything that you do, you've come to distrust your own senses and intuition.

Challenging cognitive confidence. Unfortunately, these struggles with cognitive confidence can be perpetuated by your response. When you act as if you're untrustworthy and require extra vigilance, you miss out on opportunities to test out your theory. If you check the stove six times, you learn that you are safe *precisely because* you checked the stove six times. You miss out on the opportunity to see what would have happened if you had just walked away when you were done with the stove. It's sort of like doing research with no control group. There's no comparison, no way of seeing if your results can actually be attributed to your behavior. To keep an open mind, it's important to take some risks so that you can gather additional data to form a more objective picture.

Try to identify the scenarios where you experience doubt about your perception or abilities. Do you engage in checking behaviors because you doubt yourself? Do you agonize over decisions or avoid them because you're worried you might make the wrong choice? Become a researcher and see if you can design a study to test out these beliefs. What happens when you refrain from checking? What happens when you make quick, fluid decisions without the extra analysis? Remember, if this is going to sway anyone in the scientific community, you can't rely on single case examples or anecdotes; you need a big enough sample size. So don't try this stuff once; see if you can repeat it and gather enough evidence to come to a more accurate conclusion. Focus on being open to gathering new information to see if your beliefs hold up. I'm willing to bet that, when you put more trust in yourself, you'll find that your extra analysis was unnecessary.

Beliefs About the Need to Control Thoughts

Some people greet their unwanted thoughts with a shrug and carry on with their lives; others go into containment mode, wanting to eliminate the undesirable cognitions from their awareness. Why do people treat these thoughts so differently? It partly has to do with beliefs about what these thoughts mean. If you believe that you *should* be able to control your thoughts, you're going to be more upset when they pop into your consciousness uninvited. If you believe that an upsetting thought means that you're a monster or you're going to do something awful, you're going to be more likely to treat this thought like it's a catastrophe. If you believe that your well-being depends on your ability to command your thoughts, you'll spend much more time trying to wrangle the thoughts into your control.

It helps me to visualize these concepts. Imagine that your brain is constantly hurling dodgeballs at you. Folks who don't struggle with worry are stepping back and observing. They feel no pressure to do anything in particular with these balls. Catch them or let them fall; it makes no difference. They pick up the balls only when it's strategic to do so. You, the worrier—you're scrambling all around, frantically trying to catch every ball. You're operating under the assumption that catastrophe will befall you if any were to hit the floor, if you were unable to catch each and every one. Your livelihood depends on your ability to contain and wrangle this barrage of dodgeballs.

Challenging beliefs about the need to control thoughts. You'll be happy to learn that you don't actually have to get to every ball. You don't have to catch each one, inspect it, and put it in its proper place. You have the freedom to choose any dodgeball management approach that you'd like. The problem is that your brain hasn't gotten the memo. As far as it knows, dodgeball control is an urgent task. It should be at the top of your priority list.

Here's your chance to try to show your brain another option. Try scheduling a "worry time." I know, this sounds counterproductive. You're trying to stop worrying and I'm telling you to intentionally plan for it. But hear me out: Schedule ten minutes to worry every day. An ideal time would be toward the end of the day, but not immediately before bed. Then, throughout the day, when you notice a worry, your goal is to delay worrying about it until your worry time. Acknowledge the thought, but prompt yourself to keep going and restrict worrying to the designated time. If you've been accustomed to worrying at any old time throughout the day, your brain may take some time to catch on. You may need to be persistent in reaffirming your intention.

If you could condense your worry to ten minutes per day, I think that'd be a win. But most people end up not even using their allotted time. By the time they get to it, they've forgotten what they intended to worry about. Or it just doesn't hold the same power that it did in the moment.

That said, while limiting your worry to a succinct, time-limited chunk of your day would be great, your ultimate goal in this activity is broader— you're learning that worry is not urgent and does not require your imme- diate focus. It doesn't require that you jump to attention every time it shows up or that you promptly attempt to rectify it.

Once you implement this approach, you may also try adding another step: during your worry time, say your worries out loud in front of a mirror. Most people cringe and clench their teeth when I suggest this. They instantly recognize how uncomfortable this exercise would be, how silly they would feel. While the goal is not explicitly to make you uncomfortable, it *is* to drive home just how preposterous the act of worrying can be. We often allow for bizarre or ridiculous thoughts to ping around in our heads without questioning them, but when we say them out loud and have to look ourselves in the face while doing it, most people will cut that activity short, acknowledging how senseless this whole worrying thing can be.

Cognitive Self-Consciousness

Some people are very aware of their thinking. They constantly notice their thoughts and monitor their internal experiences, paying attention to the flow of cognitions streaming through their minds. Some people have a very vocal and persistent narrator who is ever-present in their minds, and others have hardly any narrator at all.

Challenging cognitive self-consciousness. While this last metacognitive trait is not necessarily a belief, it is still an important factor in determining how you might respond to worry. If you have an internal narrator who just won't shut up, you'll likely need to cultivate a different relationship with that narrator. Think of it like having a basketball coach on the sidelines constantly barking instructions at you. When that advice is useful, it's worth listening. But when your coach is shouting nonsense, it's not worth your time. If your coach is yelling about their recipe for chicken soup or that time they went on vacation, just go ahead and focus on playing the game. If they're telling you that you suck at basketball, you should probably opt to ignore their critique. For better or worse, this is the coach you've been given and you won't get another one, but you can decide how you'd like to relate to the constant barrage of commentary and be more intentional about how you receive it. You can become a discerning consumer of your thoughts, asking yourself, *Is this thought useful? Is it relevant to what I'm doing? Is it an effective use of my time to focus on this thought right now?* You may not always be able to change the volume or frequency of these thoughts, but you can become more intentional in how you filter your attention to them. Rather than getting stuck in the content (*Is this thought true?*), focus instead on the utility (*Is this thought helpful?*).

And then, as you acquire the skill of being able to make this determination, consider how you can replace the reactions to worry thoughts with genuine strategies for living a life that's not dominated by worrying.

You Need a Strategy, Not a Reaction

You'll have no shortage of potential worries in your life. And when worrying takes over and becomes problematic, it's often because you try to solve each and every one of these problems, treating the content as if it warrants your attention every time. It's this indiscriminate approach that gets you into trouble. You keep reacting, when you need to employ a more strategic process.

Set aside the content of your worries for a moment. How would you evaluate your response to worry? Would you recommend your strategy to a friend? Do you know other people who relate differently to their worry? Is your strategy working for you? Do you even have a strategy, or do you just make it up on the fly every time and hope for the best?

Try This for Yourself. Develop a game plan for responding to worry, but don't include any content. Forget about the *worry du jour*. Financial advice is not the answer to your worry problem. It won't be solved by a more friendly boss, or a more finely tuned parenting strategy. It won't be resolved by problem-solving or "life-hacks." Your worry problem is all about how you *relate* to doubt and imperfection. And it's your relationship to your own thoughts and feelings that we're trying to enhance. How would you like to relate to worry? Consider the beliefs that we outlined in this chapter and see if you can formulate a blueprint for a style of relating to your thoughts that is better suited to your life. For example:

I want to forge a less adversarial relationship to my worry. I want to foster openness to my emotional experience and hold those feelings in perspective, while making choices about my life that are not driven by distress. I want to recognize my worry for what it is: my brain's well-intentioned but ultimately flawed effort to help me stay safe. I know that I'm capable of withstanding doubt and uncertainty. As tempting as it is, I can let go of my desire to wrangle these loose ends into my control. My worry hasn't helped me; it's only held me back. To live a life less stuck in worry, I'll need to trust in myself and relinquish those old beliefs about worry that kept me stuck.

Coming Up Next...

In the next chapter, we're going to continue our focus on process. Rather than looking at metacognitive beliefs, we'll turn our attention to meta-cognitive reasoning. How do you decide which thoughts to attend to? Are you making decisions based on the sensory information in front of you? Or the imagined simulations floating through your head? We'll explore how you can learn to spot those moments when you get absorbed into your internal experience and develop tools for bringing you back to the here and now, where you can make more adaptive choices.

CHAPTER FIVE

Connecting with Reality, Not Possibility

The world of reality has its limits; the world of imagination is boundless.

—Jean-Jacques Rousseau

We've established that you're a worrier—you fret, you obsess, you get stuck in your thoughts. But do you always do these things? Does every shred of uncertainty send you spinning off into hours of rumination? Or are there some contexts where you feel comfortable shrugging off a concern? Maybe there are even some places where you're a risk-taker. People often feel perplexed when they notice that they are perfectly capable of tolerating uncertainty in some circumstances, but not others. They can take the risk of getting behind the wheel of a car, but the comparatively safer activity of talking to a coworker induces dread and anxiety. While we can celebrate the fact that you don't worry about *everything*, the inconsistency can be maddening.

I used to work at a residential treatment program for individuals with OCD. At admission, I'd often field concerns from incoming patients about "catching" other people's symptoms (that living in a communal environment with other folks with OCD would trigger new obsessions they had never conceived of before). While this is a reasonable concern, it was, in fact, a rare occurrence. Patients were often surprised to find that someone else's obsessions just didn't do it for them. Each patient was battling their own obsession, stuck in their own unique cloud of doubt. The different iterations of worry that other patients experienced just didn't move them in the same way. Some would even express incredulousness at the obsessions of others—"How could you be worried about *that*, when you could be worried about *this*?" Each person had constructed and reinforced their own obsessions—the myriad of other worries, risks, and remote possibilities just didn't hold a candle to the one that they had built themselves.

There is randomness in the thoughts that pop into our heads. It's a mess in there. Sometimes there's not much rhyme or reason to the cacophony of mental stimuli cluttering our minds. But whether these passing thoughts get stuck and grow into obsession is a bit more systematic. The random thoughts that constantly bombard us? Meaningless. But the thoughts that get selected and developed into a constant companion of worry? That's not mere coincidence. By recognizing the process in which you build and propagate your worries, you can learn to dissolve the process before it starts.

Uncertainty Versus Doubt

Previously in this book, we've used the words *uncertainty* and *doubt* interchangeably. As we begin to pick apart how you get pulled into worry, it may be helpful to distinguish between these words. *Uncertainty* is when you don't know something, but you can get an answer. If I don't know where my keys are, I can find them, and then I know. I went from uncertain to certain. But *doubt* is when I find those keys and ask, *What if these are someone else's keys? What if another person owns the same car, same keychain, same configuration of keychain knickknacks, and somehow those keys ended up in my pocket?* With uncertainty, we go from not knowing to knowing; with doubt, we know, but we question our knowing.

In chapter 1, we discussed the idea that worrying starts as a helpful and useful process, but moves into the realm of unhelpful. Its origin in planning and analyzing can be effective, but it hits a point of diminishing returns when we miss the off-ramp and keep going. This is usually where doubt takes hold. All the signs point to "Everything is okay" but we're still focusing on remote possibilities. Instead of relying on the obvious information right in front of us, we become immersed in imagined scenarios and what-ifs. While I cringe at the often-invalidating statement of "It's all in your head," this is perhaps where there is some truth to it. More often than not, the evidence directly in front of you indicates that you're safe, while the imagined world of catastrophe resides entirely in your mind. Imagination and perception are directly in contrast.

To illustrate this divide between imagination and perception, let's do an exercise:

Imagine that you come into my office and sit down in a chair. I say, "You're going to love that chair! I've been on the waiting list for years and I finally had it shipped in from Milan this week. It's made from the finest fabrics and constructed by a master craftsman. Six generations of furniture builders have worked to refine the perfect design and they only make three chairs a year. The wood is harvested from a rare grove of trees in the Italian countryside. And the fabric is handmade by artisan weavers, using hypoallergenic materials and organic filling. You'll be the first person to ever sit in this chair." You'd probably feel pretty good about sitting down in that chair. You might even feel special to get the opportunity to sit in such a spectacular, majestic chair.

But what if I said this, instead: "Um, you might want to sit at your own risk. It's a long story, but I had to drop some things off at the dump the other day and I saw this chair sitting there. I needed one for my office, so I threw it in the back of a moving van. It smelled kind of funky, so I kept it in my garage for a few days to air out, but then my kid was playing on it and I think something may have escaped her diaper, because the chair was kind of damp afterward. There were some bugs on it too, but don't worry, I doused it in insecticide before you came, so it should probably be fine."

That second one might feel a little different, right? Same chair, two different stories. As you might guess, the reality of the chairs in my office is pretty far from either of these stories. I have decent chairs, kept reasonably clean, vaguely stylish, sat on by a moderate amount of people. Nothing to write home about. But these stories create a different experience. The idea here is not to decide which one is true or false; it's to notice how storytelling affects our experience of things. When we create a vivid and immersive story, we can get lost in it and the story begins to color how we navigate and experience the world around us. Our capacity to create immersive, lived-in stories about the world can pull us out of the here and now and into a fictionalized account of our surroundings.

Try This for Yourself. Use everyday items around you—a dinner plate, your phone, a doorknob, and so forth—and create backstories. Imagine the filth and muck that may have befallen these poor, downtrodden items. Imagine the pristine, cherished, charmed life that they may have lived. Notice how these immersive stories change how you relate to the items. While the objective reality of the items remains the same, the subjective interpretation changes.

When you get hijacked by these internal stories, pulled in by the realistic fiction of your mind, it's called *imaginal absorption*. You're lost, swallowed up by the plausible smoke and mirrors of your mind's creative power. This isn't always bad—you do a version of this when you read a book or daydream or listen to a story. Consider what it's like when you're watching a really scary movie—you get tense, your heart pounds, you might startle or shriek in moments when something unexpected happens. Of course, you recognize that you're not in danger, but you've become absorbed into this imagined world and it starts to blur with reality. You respond as if you're in danger. It *feels* real.

So, how is it that you get tricked into responding to the imagined world of your worry rather than the reality in front of you? Well, let's imagine that the scary movie you watched is *Jaws* and now you're about to get in the ocean. I'm willing to bet that your thoughts are going to turn toward sharks. Your assessment of the situation might even change a bit. You may be more likely to align your behavior with the world of *Jaws*, in which man-eating sharks are constantly prowling the ocean, rather than the here and now, where shark attacks are rarer than getting struck by lightning. You might be scanning for that dorsal fin sticking out of the water. You might hesitate to go too far from shore. The objective reality has not changed, but the richness of the world of *Jaws* has started to infiltrate reality, or rather, your interpretation of reality. The fear, the images, the possibility—they make it hard to stay grounded in the here and now.

O'Connor and Aardema (2012) call this *inferential confusion*, and it's the basis for inference-based therapy (IBT). Inferential confusion is when you reason and make choices based on imagination, mistaking hypothetical possibility for reality. Absorption into your inner life obscures your ability to distinguish between what's actually happening and the vast array of infinite possibilities in your mind. The story you've concocted is now treated as reality, used as a basis for decision-making and strategy even though nothing about the present moment substantiates your fear. We all do this to some extent, though for folks who struggle with anxiety, this process can become problematic, as actions based on inferential confusion perpetuate the anxiety cycle.

In addition to the experience of imaginal absorption, IBT identifies several faulty reasoning errors that contribute to inferential confusion—and it provides guidance to get you thinking about what the evidence of your situation actually indicates.

Supporting Evidence

Let's look at some of the reasoning errors that might perpetuate the doubt, *What if I get eaten by a shark?*:

- Abstract facts. *Shark attacks do happen.*

- General rules. *I should be careful when swimming in the ocean.*

- Hearsay. *I saw a story in the news about a shark attack.*

- Personal experience. *I got stung by a jellyfish once. And pinched by a hermit crab. I even got rammed in the stomach by a goat at a petting zoo as a kid* (all true stories). *Animals attack me!*

- Possibility. *I could be the unlucky person who gets attacked by a shark.*

Notice that none of the above statements are untrue. There is a certain logic and credibility here, which is what makes them so compelling in the presence of doubt. Ultimately, it's not the truth of these statements that's problematic; it's the relevance. They're taken out of context, used as a justification for a feared outcome. You become absorbed in what you fear and then use faulty reasoning to validate your choices. You can think of this kind of like doing really bad scientific research. If I'm a lazy or unscrupulous researcher, I might come up with a hypothesis and then seek out only the evidence that supports that hypothesis. I'm starting with a conclusion and then working backward to manufacture evidence for it. If I really care about sound science, I'm instead going to allow my actual observations to drive my conclusion. If the observations don't support the hypothesis, then it's likely false. Again, we're talking about process, not content. Even though these statements (content) may be true, the process (faulty reasoning errors) is flawed.

Let's walk through a couple more examples:

Doubt: *What if the moon landing was a hoax?*

- Abstract facts. *The government does keep secrets.*

- General rules. *You shouldn't blindly trust others.*

- Hearsay. *My uncle's roommate said Neil Armstrong isn't really an astronaut.*

- Personal experience. *I've been fooled before.*

- Possibility. *I wasn't on the moon personally, so I can't rule it out.*

Okay, I know this one's a bit more outlandish, but when you look at the *reasoning process*, your worries are no better than conspiracy theories! Again, every last bit of the content above could be true, but as a system of reasoning, it's still a pile of garbage. Let's do one more:

Doubt: *What if my boss hates me and I'm going to get fired?*

- Abstract facts. *People get fired all the time.*

- General rules. *If your boss doesn't like you, your job may be at risk.*

- Hearsay. *My coworkers said that a past employee was fired.*

- Personal experience. *At my performance review, my boss gave me feedback about things I can improve.*

- Possibility. *I can't be assured that I'll never be fired.*

When you start with a doubt, then work backward to build supporting evidence, you're going to end up in a state of inferential confusion, absorbed in your imagination to such a degree that you start responding to this internal simulation rather than the reality in front of you. Your reasoning process gives credibility to the doubt, even when it's not earned.

Try This for Yourself. Identify a doubt that you struggle with. As in the preceding examples, you can usually tap into your doubt by starting with a what-if statement. Then, using the five faulty reasoning errors, find the ways that you have justified and rationalized your doubt. You can use a piece of paper or download a blank copy of this exercise at the publisher's website for this book: http://www.newharbinger.com/52144.

While the initial thought may have been random, the doubt that grew from it was at least partially constructed by your own reasoning approach. Next, see what it's like to repeat this exercise with someone else's worry, something that doesn't bother you. Just like we practiced creating different backstories for household items and noticed how these varied stories impacted our experience, we can also practice noticing how our reasoning errors can start to construct obsessional doubt.

Know Your Vulnerability

In exposure-based approaches to anxiety, we're often interested in identifying your *core fear*. This is the thing at the heart of your worry, several layers deep. It's not, *What if my boss hates me?*—it's, *What if I'm awful and unlovable?* In IBT, there's a similar idea, called your *vulnerable-self theme*. It's a feared version of yourself. The Mr. Hyde to your Dr. Jekyll. The person you don't want to be. It's helpful to identify this theme, as it's another factor that drives inferential confusion and obsessional doubt. It leaves you primed for your particular brand of worry. This is part of why you don't slip into worrying about any old doubt that shows up; you build obsessional doubt to avoid becoming this unwanted version of yourself.

Try This for Yourself. Take a moment and see if you can identify your vulnerable-self theme. Who do you fear you'd become if you stopped worrying? What are the traits or characteristics of the person you're scared to become? What sources of information have you been using to assess how you stack up against this diabolical-evil-twin self?

I'm often struck by the paradoxical nature of the vulnerable self-theme—folks who worry about being irresponsible are often the most diligent, those who worry about hurting others are often the most conscientious, and people who worry about acting impulsively are often the most restrained. There is a marked discrepancy between the outward reality and the way that you perceive yourself. This comes back to inferential confusion again—you're assessing your character based on imagined possibility and out-of-context facts, rather than basing your assessment on what's happening right in front of you. In short: You doubt reality and trust imagination.

For example, if your vulnerable-self theme is that you might harm others due to your negligence, you might become mired in doubt by paying attention to the following variables:

Doubt: *What if I become someone who is negligent and causes harm to others?*

- Abstract facts. *The Titanic sank because someone wasn't paying enough attention.*

- General rules. *It's your responsibility to prevent harm if you can.*

- Hearsay. *I read a news story about someone who fell asleep at the wheel and their family died in a crash.*

- Personal experience. *I've made mistakes when I'm tired. I've cut corners when I'm in a hurry.*

- Possibility. *It's possible that a lapse in judgment or attention will have catastrophic consequences.*

As you can see, doubt is constructed about not only possible feared outcomes, but also the very nature of who you are. In this example, if you respond to your doubt by overcompensating with excessive vigilance, planning, or checking, you are reinforcing the belief that you are teetering on the precipice of becoming that feared self and that these behaviors are the only things standing between you and breaking bad.

Instead, try this: Consider how businesses conduct employee reviews. Rather than simply relying on employee self-report or even customer ratings, many businesses use a 360-degree review. They ask for feedback from the employee, their supervisor, their direct reports, their colleagues, and so forth. This process recognizes the subjectivity of using only a single reviewer and cultivates a fairer, more comprehensive picture by diversifying the sources. Imagine if your boss was writing your review and throughout the process someone was whispering in her ear, "He's a horrible employee. He's irresponsible and dumb and he never does anything right." You wouldn't feel too optimistic about your review, would you? Your boss's opinion could be swayed. Well, your assessment of your own character is also susceptible to bias. You have critical thoughts swirling around, doubts about what could be bombarding your mind. It requires effort to zoom out and consider what kinds of information you want to pay attention to. If you're worried that your boss hates you, should you put more stock in the direct feedback from your boss, or the imagined scenario in your mind in which your boss secretly harbors ill feelings? Similarly, how do you want to assess your character? What kinds of factors do you want to take into account? And which kinds of fears about yourself or your life are you aware of that might skew your impression of yourself?

But isn't this reassurance? Not exactly. Reassurance would be saying, "No, I'm sure your boss thinks you're amazing!" In truth, I have no idea what your boss thinks of you. For all I know, they think you're awful. The goal here is not to give you false platitudes; it's to get you to be intentional about *how* you gather information and to ensure that you're doing it in a thoughtful yet rigorous way. Essentially, if you think you're an awful employee, we want it to be because you have ample evidence of that being true in the real, external world (missing deadlines, being late, etc.), and not because of a bunch of out-of-context facts or imagined narratives (your boss gave you a funny look). You'd be amazed at how often we come to conclusions about ourselves and the world around us without performing some basic due diligence to reality-test our beliefs.

Putting It All Together

The processes we considered in this chapter—imaginal absorption, inferential confusion, vulnerable-self themes, and other products of the tendency we sometimes have to confuse imagination for perception—come together in a perfect storm to perpetuate anxiety and worry. Your vulnerable-self theme leaves you susceptible to certain kinds of thoughts or triggers. Your fear of becoming this awful version of yourself puts you on defense and you're more likely to rely on faulty logic and reasoning, which in turn fuels imaginal absorption and results in inferential confusion, whereby you start treating this imagined possibility as reality.

I know, that's a lot. Here's an example that brings all of these processes together: Each night when I go to bed, I plan to sleep through the night until my alarm goes off in the morning. Call me crazy, but I've decided that's the best strategy when it comes to sleep. I have young kids, so my plan doesn't always come to fruition. Someone has a bad dream, someone has an accident, someone's blanket is bunched up and a professional grown-up's blanket-straightening skills are needed. Sadly, my sleep-through-the-night plan does not always go off without a hitch, but still, I stick by it as an optimal strategy. Now, sometimes in one of these middle-of-the-night moments, I'll have a thought: *What if an intruder is in the closet? What if someone is under the bed? Or in the shower?* Sometimes a vision will accompany the thought—a scene out of a slasher film, perhaps. Sometimes a pang of fear will arise. Or a mental admonishment that I should protect my family, packaged with a sprinkling of guilt. By now, you can probably rattle off some of the reasoning errors that could support this doubt:

Doubt: *What if someone has broken into our house and is going hurt us?*

- Abstract facts. *People are murdered every day in our country.*

- General rules. *If you can protect your family by doing something simple, you should.*

- Hearsay. *I saw on the news that there was a break-in recently in a neighboring town.*

- Personal experience. *There have been times when I've forgotten to lock the door.*

- Possibility. *Maybe that kid I was mean to in third grade is coming back to exact revenge.*

You could probably also pick out the vulnerable-self theme: *What if I'm the kind of person who is too scared to protect their family?* Notice it's not simply a fear of an outcome—*I don't want to be murdered*—it's about who I might be. For some reason, my impulse in these moments is to check—behind the shower curtain, under the bed, in the closet. I suppose if there really were an intruder quietly lurking in my closet, I'd probably fare better if I just left them alone and went back to sleep, crossing my fingers that they just needed to borrow a sweater. I suspect that surprising the would-be murderer would probably be a good way to be murdered, but nonetheless, my impulse is usually to check. Just to be sure. The thoughts, the fear, the guilt, the reasoning, the vulnerable-self—it's enough to make the moment feel "real." It's immersive, like watching a movie. The vividness and texture of the experience pull me away from the present moment. In the present moment, though, I didn't hear any glass shattering. The alarm didn't go off. The dog didn't bark. There were no muddy footprints across the floor. No lights turned on. Nothing about it indicates that I'm in any danger. Nothing supports the decision to shift away from my original plan of sleeping through the night. After all, I didn't set my alarm for 3 a.m., deciding that it would be prudent to perform my nightly check for burglars. That wasn't part of the plan. So why would I do it now? Just because a thought popped up? Because I could imagine possible catastrophe? Because for a brief moment some hypothetical unknown possibility floated up to the surface of my mind and grabbed my attention?

In moments of imaginal absorption, it can be helpful to bring yourself back to the here and now. By grounding yourself in the present moment, you can better assess your surroundings. Did you actually see a shark in the water? Did your boss give you harsh feedback? Are there signs of a break-in? Do you have direct information from the world around you that supports your doubt? Or has that doubt been constructed based on imagined possibility?

In many ways, this whole chapter has been an exercise in learning to trust yourself. It's learning to trust in your senses, your intuition, and your ability to remain in the moment and make moment-to-moment choices, without the need for analysis or mental simulations. When you cross the street, you allow your senses—the sound or appearance of an oncoming car—to guide you. Your ability to imagine a collision or your recollection of disastrous car-accident stories do not have any bearing on your in-the-moment decision to cross or not cross. In fact, to allow those things to inform your decision would probably be a bit reckless.

As we discussed in the previous chapter, the goal here is to get away from content. In that chapter, you learned to build awareness of metacognitive beliefs, challenging the unhelpful beliefs that perpetuate anxiety and worry. Here, we're similarly building awareness, though this time it's about the reasoning process that drives anxiety by constructing doubt in the first place. We're looking at the sources of evidence you're using to determine your response. Just like a jury would have a hard time convicting someone based on circumstantial evidence or hearsay, you too can make an effort to maintain standards about how you reason your way to a conclusion.

I'm reminded of the famous thought experiment about Schrödinger's cat. The details of this paradox involve quantum physics and go far beyond our purposes, but the short version is that Schrödinger described an experiment in which a cat is sealed in a box with something lethal. Schrödinger envisioned a decaying radioactive isotope that would register on a Geiger counter and signal the release of noxious gas, though let's just call it poisoned cat food, for simplicity's sake. At the end of an hour, you can open the box and find the cat alive or dead. But as long as the box is sealed, both possibilities exist. Similarly, your fears will remain in a perpetual state of ambiguity as long as they remain in your head. You can turn them over as many times as you want, just as you can imagine both outcomes for Schrödinger's poor cat. You can't think your way out of imagined possibility. Instead, your goal is to come back to the moment and open the box by recentering in the here and now. The problem is not the existence of doubt—it's your determination to resolve that doubt in your imagination rather than out in the world.

Coming Up Next...

In the next chapter, as you continue to put the metacognitive tools we've learned to work, you'll learn how clarifying and moving toward your values can help you live a life that's aligned with what's important to you, rather than allowing your worries or anxiety to determine your actions.

CHAPTER SIX

Living Your Values, Not Thinking Them

*If we have our own why in life, we shall get along with
almost any how.*

—Friedrich Nietzsche, *Twilight of the Idols*

Worrying has a way of masquerading as something else. It can seem like it's helping you solve a problem, but then you end up ruminating, stuck in indecision. It can seem like it's helping you prepare for catastrophe, but then you get overwhelmed and anxious with anticipation. This mutation—from helpful tool to fruitless endeavor—is one of the more insidious aspects of worrying.

And this problem can even go a step further. The origin in something well intentioned and useful leads to the false belief that worrying is beneficial—that it's a protective force ensuring that you are safe. This is one of the "positive beliefs" about worrying that we discussed in chapter 4.

One aspect of this belief can be especially problematic: the belief that worrying is keeping you in line with your values. This might show up as:

- *If I don't worry, what kind of person would I be?*

- *How can I be responsible and caring if I don't worry?*

- *Doesn't my worrying show my loved ones that they're important to me?*

It can sometimes seem like the purpose of worrying is to operationalize your values—a way to demonstrate your love and care. But worrying is self-serving. It's for you, not for others. Worrying is an (unhelpful) way to regulate your emotions, to *feel* like you're caring. If you worry about your kid who has stayed out too late, are you actually protecting them? Does your worrying change the outcome? Or is it just a way for you to mentally grapple with uncertainty and fear? In that situation, there's not much that you can do within the confines of your head that will change the outcome. You could call your child, track their phone, call their friends, or form a search party. But all of that just gives you more information about what's happening; it doesn't change what's happened. Actual prevention strategies—imparting good values and judgment, spending time practicing driving at night, curating a trusting relationship with your child so they feel safe asking for help—would have already been done in the past. All of these things can avert danger, but they cannot be performed in the moment. It's too late for that. So instead, you worry. In the absence of effective tools, you'll settle for ineffective ones and do your best to maintain the delusion that you're doing something useful, that you're exercising care. You want to be a good parent and worrying seems like the quickest path to your goal, but really, it's you attempting to find an answer, to placate your fear.

This is where values come in. Values can help you find a compass to guide you through difficult moments. When you choose to align your behavior with something ephemeral, like passing thoughts and feelings, it's like steering a ship based on the clouds. There's no true course, no direction. The clouds will drift and so will your ship's course. But when you navigate with something solid and fixed—a compass or the North Star—you can find consistent direction. When you align your behavior with your values, you'll ensure that you stay on course, even as the emotional clouds shift and move around you. So the question isn't, *Is my kid okay?* It's, *What kind of parent do I want to be? Do I want to be trusting? How can I demonstrate care and concern in a way that's consistent with who I want to be? What balance of helping versus fostering independence will be the most useful for my child?* Ultimately, values are about stepping back and assessing how you want to show up in the world and for the people around you.

What Are Values?

Values are the guiding principles that inform who you want to be. Just as a blueprint guides construction of a house, values allow us to navigate the world in a way that's consistent with who we are. Values are how we make meaning, find fulfillment, and actualize the person we aspire to be. Values are not goals. They're not accomplishments. In fact, values are not achievable at all; they're who and how you want to be. For example, as I'm typing, my goal might be to write a book, but my value could be helping others.

Goals	Values
Specific, measurable, achievable	Subjective, not achievable
Something you do	A principle you embody
Can be accomplished	On-going, indefinite
Helpful tool to break down and operationalize values	Helpful to provide direction
Example: Graduating from college	Example: curiosity, mastery, responsibility

When our kids were younger, every time my wife and I would go out and leave them with a babysitter, we'd leave instructions. The instructions were always overly long and detailed and probably went unread by most of the babysitters. They contained advice like, "The kids like a story and song before bed," or "Don't forget to turn on the white noise machine," or "If the dog begs for food, just ignore her. She's been fed, she just has an insatiable appetite." These instructions served as a way to try to make the evening go as smoothly as possible, to minimize the potential for babysit-ter distress or child rebellion. But they weren't really a blueprint for how to raise our kids. They were just a stopgap measure aimed at getting through the night without hassle.

How might those instructions look if they were aimed at the long term? What if, instead of being instructions for a babysitter, they were directives in our will for a caregiver? It'd probably read more like, "Try to demonstrate kindness even when it's hard," or "Encourage the kids to pursue their passions," or "They'll lose their inheritance if they ever become a Yankees fan." Okay, maybe not that last one. But you get the idea. The babysitter instructions are about ease and comfort. The will instructions are a blueprint for living by a set of values. They abandon the comparatively insignificant details about the day-to-day, instead prioritiz-ing the things that truly matter.

That said, it can be challenging to pivot to prioritizing values. Many of us are more accustomed to thinking about goals. We're more comfort-able thinking about concrete accomplishments or aspirational circum-stances. We get stuck focusing on "*What* do you want to be when you grow up?" rather than "*Who* do you want to be?" This can be so ingrained that many people struggle to even identify what their values are. They return to "I want a family" or "I want to be a lawyer" rather than "I care about connecting with others" or "It's important to make the world more just." It can help to spend some time clarifying your values.

Identifying Your Values

Sometimes it can be hard to nail down what's really important to us. There are so many different principles and moral standards that it can feel overwhelming to try to find some rhyme or reason to it all. One way to get a handle on your values is to do a sorting activity.

Make a list of values. You can use the list on the following page as a starting point, but feel free to add your own. Write each value down on a separate piece of paper or index card. I know it's tempting to skip this step and just do it all in your head, but I promise it will be more effective when you actually force yourself to wrestle with this a bit. Next, sort the cards into three categories: Very Important, Important, and Not Important. These rankings are not permanent. They're not legally binding, either, so be bold and make the tough choices. You may change your mind, your answers may change over time, and that's all fine.

Acceptance	Excellence	Personal Growth
Achievement	Fairness	Power
Adaptability	Family	Pride
Adventurousness	Flexibility	Punctuality
Altruism	Friendliness	Recognition
Ambition	Frugality	Respect
Assertiveness	Fun	Responsibility
Authenticity	Generosity	Safety
Belonging	Gratitude	Self-Confidence
Bravery	Honesty	Self-Knowledge
Commitment	Humility	Self-Reliance
Communication	Inclusiveness	Self-Respect
Compassion	Innovation	Service
Cooperation	Integrity	Skillfulness
Courage	Loyalty	Spirituality
Creativity	Nature	Sustainability
Curiosity	Novelty	Tradition
Dependability	Order	Trustworthiness
Diversity	Passion	Uniqueness
Education	Patience	Usefulness
Efficiency	Perseverance	Wealth

Notice where perhaps you hold onto conflicting values—you value independence *and* connection with others; or you want to be creative or flexible, while also valuing order and responsibility. You may find that your predicaments in life, the dilemmas that send you into a tailspin of analysis, can be attributed to these incongruent values. If I value honesty, I should tell my friend that I can't stand their new haircut; but if I value caring for others, I should spare them that hurt and keep it to myself. If I value achievement, I should do everything I can to nail that project at work; but if I value sustainability, I should prioritize rest and balance.

It's tempting in these moments to try to figure out which one to pick, to select the "right" answer. But the truth is that we have a finite amount of time and we have to make some compromises. We have to navigate a single path through life, wishing that we could somehow choose both options. And we must accept some degree of disappointment, knowing that no choice will perfectly capture every nook and cranny of our values. We'll have inconsistencies, holes we wish we could fill. It's not right or wrong, but rather, two choices both containing a unique set of pros and cons.

I wish that I could spend more time with friends. I value relationships and connecting with others. But I also know that I'm in a season of life where a lot of my energy is going to go toward my young kids, and that investment will inevitably come at the cost of other things that are important to me. This is a zero-sum game—one choice comes at the cost of another. Just like you, I wish that I could rip open the fabric of the universe so that I could make both choices at once. But alas, I'll need to meander my way through life, selecting one imperfect action after another.

Your values-sorting activity is a good way to provide some direction. It's not a perfect formula, but ideally our lives will reflect our values to some degree. The time we spend on tasks will be proportionate to how important those things are to us. You may not feel a surge of relief and peace when you've made your choice; you may still pine for that world in which you get to make both choices. But you'll need to carry that pain with you as you forge a path, knowing that you'll get where you need to go if you use your values as a guide.

Moving Toward or Away from Your Values

One of the biggest missteps that I see in my practice is that clients often believe that eliminating unwanted thoughts or feelings is a prerequisite for living the life that they want. If they can just conquer those pesky emotions, all of the doors will open and they'll finally be able to pursue their dreams. Sadly, your brain contains an endless supply of thoughts and feelings. You can no more conquer them than Sisyphus can get his rock to the top of the mountain. The more you try, the more your time and energy are diverted away from your life. The best approach is to reverse this paradigm rather than waiting for your thoughts and feelings to abate before living your life, instead, go after your life first. Let the thoughts and feelings come as they will, but don't allow this ebb and flow to dictate the course of the life you build for yourself.

Believe it or not, I've worked with clients who have said that successful treatment actually meant that they experienced *more* anxiety! This is because they became more willing to live their lives on their own terms, more open to taking risks and embracing the discomfort that followed. They no longer shied away from challenges out of fear of anxiety. You see, more anxiety is not synonymous with more dysfunction. It's possible to be someone who is prone to feeling more anxious and yet still live a life aligned with what's meaningful and important. You've probably been inundated with messages telling you to make it all feel better—get instant relief from your symptoms, live a blissful, sunny, drug-commercial life. But no one can maintain that euphoric state permanently. We're all going to feel pain, sadness, and anxiety. It's simply part of our existence here on Earth. Our best bet is to learn to coexist with that pain and to minimize its impact by moving toward what's important to us. Each and every one of our actions takes us closer or further from our values. Each moment is a choice point where you get to decide how you construct your life—do you use values as your blueprint? Or something else?

Let's consider the value of being a good friend. What kinds of things might move you toward that value? What would move you away from it?

Toward	Away
Being present while spending time with friends	Canceling plans
Being responsive to communication	Being flaky about responding to texts
Giving support, in addition to receiving it	Excessively seeking reassurance or advice
Practicing kindness and care for others	Immersing yourself in your internal experience at the cost of attending to others

Try This for Yourself. Using one of the values that you've identified, make a list of some of your toward and away moves. You can use a piece of paper or download a blank copy of a Values Planner at the publisher's website for this book: http://www.newharbinger.com/52144. What are you currently doing to bring you closer to embodying that value? What do you do that moves you away from it? What would you need to be willing to do to align your actions with your values? Would you need to be willing to experience uncomfortable emotions? Would you need to be open to situations that might trigger uncomfortable thoughts or doubts? How would life look if you always responded to discomfort by moving away from your values? What would it look like if you always moved toward them?

Acting On Your Values

Even after sorting out your values, it can be challenging to figure out how to apply them. How do you take these nebulous concepts and translate them into action? In this part of the chapter, we'll discuss ways of rendering your values into something more tangible.

Trying On Your Values

Goals are actionable behaviors that move you toward a value. If your value is creativity, for example, you could make a goal of painting. The corresponding behaviors could be signing up for a painting class, buying some painting supplies, talking to a friend who is an artist, or going to an art museum for inspiration. Those big, overarching values can feel sort of daunting, and it can help to dismantle them so that you can get to the smaller, component parts.

To get started, though, you'll need to begin with a goal. Rather than getting stuck figuring out if a behavior will bring you joy or fulfillment, simply do it first. Let yourself be immersed in it. Be curious and open, allowing for the nonjudgmental experience of the behavior. Whatever specific thing you choose to do, think of it like an experiment. Allow yourself to be present and engaged in the activity. There will be plenty of time to assess if this activity fulfills you, so when you're in the activity itself, try to let go of the analysis for a bit. You may decide that this is a great fit for you or may ultimately decide that you missed the mark, but the important thing is that you don't let making the "right" choice prevent you from taking action. This emphasis on choosing the "right" activities—the perfect hobby, the right career, the ideal partner—often prevents us from taking action. It's a hurdle, raising the bar so high that we never get started. When you start moving toward your values, it's important that you make yourself open to new things and uncomfortable experiences, trusting that your compass will ultimately lead you in the right direction. So don't get bogged down in the details; focus on doing the activity with fewer strings attached. A great way to ensure that you don't enjoy an activity is to spend your time assessing whether you're enjoying the activity. Instead, just get open, get curious, and let yourself have the experience.

Acting On Your Values When It's Complicated

When you discover those things that are important to you, you may find that worry starts to take hold. It's one thing to dismiss worry when it shows up in trivial or meaningless places, but what do you do when it starts to infiltrate the things you really care about?

Let's say, for example, that you value being a conscientious person and so you worry about climate change. Is global warming a problem? Absolutely! But do you have to start solving that problem every time the thought arises? Do you need to scramble to recycle a bottle every time you have a thought about global warming? Nope. You are in charge of how and when you respond to this problem. You can find an approach that fits your values. You may indeed have values that align with this worry—you feel it's important to take care of our planet or you value caring for future generations. You can act with intention, deciding which mitigation strategies you'll employ to live a life in congruence with these values.

You will, however, need to accept that you'll have to draw a line somewhere. You can't do everything. You can't save the planet single-handedly. So, you'll have to decide how much space you have in your life for this problem. How do you build it into your life proportionately so that you're attending to it, while also caring for the other competing values? I want to minimize my carbon footprint, but I also live in a place without reliable public transportation, and so I need a minivan to cart around my kids. I care about the planet, but I also care about providing some level of convenience for my family. Your acceptance of where you draw your line is important because each time your thoughts show up and try to drag you back to solving this problem, you need to be able to hold that line. You don't answer to your thoughts—you answer to your values. Your job is to examine how your values prescribe that you attend to this problem.

I like to imagine a spectrum: on one end of this spectrum, I live in a Styrofoam palace, burning old plastic to keep warm and dumping my garbage into the ocean; on the other end, I'm Thoreau on Walden Pond, generating zero waste, zero emissions—just a man in the woods. In between these extremes are a million permutations of how I might live in recognition of our warming planet. Each point on the spectrum is a compromise, moving both toward and away from competing values. Every step toward caring for the planet is a step away from convenience and comfort. I wish I could tell you that it's neater, that by turning it over in your head enough you'll be able to reduce it to an easy choice where you get to have it all. But sometimes we need to make hard, imperfect choices. In fact, I'll go a step further—*every* choice we make fits this mold; every action is a compromise. The best we can do is to make the hard, imperfect choices that are in synergy with our balanced values.

Try This for Yourself. Identify one of your common worries. Notice where this concern does indeed overlap with your values. Something about this worry is meaningful and important to you. Next, grab a piece of paper and draw a line, labeling each end of the line with the extremes, as we did in the example above. At each point on this spectrum, your chosen response will come at the expense of another value or concern. This is true for every single concern that you have, every value that you hold. You'll have to make a choice about where to draw the line, ensuring that you're not only attending to this value, but holding it in balance with your other values. Now, see if you can make a value-informed choice about how to respond to this problem. Intentionally acknowledge the compromise you'll need to make—this may evoke painful feelings, perhaps regret that you can't do it all. You can *both* feel these feelings *and* align your behavior with the balanced equation of values that fits your life. And remember, not making a choice is a choice too. If you spend your time stuck in analysis, that is time spent moving away from actually living in accordance with your values.

Acting On Your Values When It's Hard

One of my kids is really into dragons. Like, *really* into dragons. Dragon books, dragon figurines, dragon shows and movies, dragon games. She could talk to me about dragons for hours. Now, I like dragons as much as the next guy, but I can start to lose interest. You could say I get bored sometimes. Maybe you could even say that sometimes I really don't want to hear about dragons anymore. Ever again. So, when I go to put my kid to bed and she wants to tell me all about how the *Slitherwing* dragon is different than the *Snafflefang* dragon, what do you think I do? Do I tell her I'm bored? Do I yawn and tell her that I'm using every ounce of self-control to maintain interest? No, I don't. Because my feelings are actually not what's important in that moment. Of course, my feelings are valid and there are certainly situations where my feelings might be more integral to the experience. But here, my feelings are not what's meaningful about this interaction. What's important is showing my kid that I support her passions. It's being present and showing her through my actions that she's important to me. It's encouraging her curiosity and excitement in sharing her world with me. It's about who I want to be as a parent, not whether I'm invigorated by the conversation.

It's easy to get lost in the thoughts and feelings of an experience. It's frustrating when unwanted thoughts or uncomfortable emotions mar an activity. We can get hung up on the inefficiencies, the mistakes, or the details that didn't work out. But it's worthwhile to ask yourself, *Were those things important for this experience?* If I'm in charge of the nuclear reactor, then yes, I would probably want to put a premium on not making mistakes. But if I'm taking a trip to the beach and I forget the beach chairs? Or I get sand in the car? That's not really what was important about the beach! It wasn't an exercise in perfection—it was a way to spend time with my family or to connect with nature or to practice surfing. Our thoughts often pull us into details, and it's important to remember to use a critical lens in determining whether those details are actually important or relevant to our values.

Try This for Yourself. While it's great to apply this filter in the moment, it can sometimes be even more helpful to practice it *before* an activity. If, before I put my kid to sleep, I remind myself of what's important about that interaction, I'm going to be much more likely to stay within my values and much less likely to get sucked into the thoughts and feelings that arise. If you're prone to worrying about details, mistakes, or planning, try making a "Top Three List" before you do an activity. What are the top three most important things about the experience? What are the underlying values that you're connecting with by doing this thing? Affirm these values *before* you engage in an activity. This will help you align with what matters while giving yourself permission to let go of the details that don't make the Top Three cut. Here's what that might look like for my dragon fanatic's bedtime routine:

1. *Show her that she's important by being present.* Value: connection, care for others

2. *Demonstrate interest by asking questions and listening to answers.* Value: curiosity, flexibility, patience

3. *Be kind.* Value: care for others, creating an environment for my child to thrive

Each of the above items will require some sacrifice. I'll have to be present during bedtime, even though it's the end of my day and I'm ready to check out. I'll have to stay engaged in the conversation, even though I might be feeling bored or tired. I'll have to demonstrate kindness, even though I may feel frustrated. These lingering thoughts and feelings are part of the experience, an unavoidable part of a messy life. Rather than trying to resolve that messiness, you can relate to it differently by putting it in perspective, noticing the mess that matters and the mess that doesn't. You won't always nail it (I certainly don't), but bringing your values into the equation will help to prioritize the things you care about while jettisoning the unimportant details that would occupy your time.

Coming Up Next...

This section of the book has focused on building awareness and changing the way that you relate to thoughts—whether in noticing unhelpful beliefs about thoughts (chapter 4), identifying the process that leaves you immersed in thoughts (chapter 5), or in this chapter, distinguishing thoughts from valued action. The next section will shift from how you *relate* to thoughts to how you *respond* to thoughts. We'll use behavioral principles to help you develop strategies to disengage from rumination and anxiety.

PART III

Challenging Worry

CHAPTER SEVEN

Using Response Prevention for Worry

One thorn of experience is worth a whole wilderness of warning.

—James Russell Lowell, *Among My Books*

We're all locked into our own perception, to some degree. Our experience occurs within the confines of our minds, making us unable to view the world from any perspective other than our own. What happens inside our heads is uniquely ours. As a result, many of us don't stop to nail down our internal experiences, assigning names or labels to these mental phenomena. We experientially know how our minds work; we know what happens in our heads when we're lying in bed, going to sleep, but without the ability to directly compare our mental processes to someone else's, we often allow these internal experiences to remain fuzzy and nondescript.

To begin engaging with your mind in more effective ways, it will be helpful to identify these mental processes more precisely. By refining these concepts and giving them names, it will allow you to differentiate between the parts that you can control and the parts that you can't—the parts that will be helpful and the ones that will waste your time. We'll focus in particular on three components: *awareness, attention,* and *engagement.*

Awareness

Awareness is the broadest of these terms; it's our capacity to notice. Awareness is our mind's recognition of the wide range of input bombarding our brains from moment to moment. As we make our way through life, information constantly floats in and out of our awareness. You can think of this as raw data—unanalyzed, unfocused, meaningless by itself without some interpretation. It's the external stimuli that wander into our mind's viewfinder—our surroundings, environment, situations. But it's also the internal—noticing our sensory experiences, thoughts, feelings, desires, urges, and bodily sensations. It's sort of a full-body scan, without a doctor to interpret. A snapshot without a caption to provide context.

You do not have the ability to control your awareness. You can become *aware of your awareness* (noticing that you're having a thought, for example) and you can decide how you'd like to respond to that awareness, but you don't control the initial burst of mental information that pops into your brain. Your goal is not to attempt to control these perceptual comings and goings, but rather, to allow the natural ebb and flow to occur without intervention. It doesn't mean you'll enjoy every single thought that enters your mind or every uncomfortable sensation that you become aware of, but simply that you'll notice these pieces of information and acknowledge the futility of trying to change or control them.

Sometimes you won't be thrilled with the stuff that enters your awareness. The annoying song that grabs your attention while you're trying to work, the upsetting images that arise and evoke distress, the remembrance of a funny joke during a somber moment. It's natural to feel frustrated by these experiences, to want them to go away.

Before we move on, I want to explain the difference between *distraction* and *Distraction*. The first (distraction) is an unintentional experience—getting pulled away, losing focus, unintentionally having one's mind pivot to something new, exciting, or stimulating. This is harmless, if annoying. We all weed through distractions when we're trying to focus.

The second (Distraction) is an intentional effort to avoid by controlling your awareness. It's when you're feeling anxiety or you have an uncomfortable thought and you try to push that experience away by immersing yourself in a different experience. You Distract yourself so that you don't have to face something hard. This is harmful. When you Distract as a means of avoidance, you're reinforcing the anxiety cycle by acting as if the thoughts are dangerous or unmanageable.

Furthermore, not only is it impossible to control your awareness, but efforts to do so will usually have the opposite effect. The act of *thought suppression*—intentionally trying *not* to have a thought—makes it *more likely* that you will have that thought. It's kind of like telling your brain, "Don't fall off that cliff," part of your brain is now vigilant about the cliff. It's putting more attention on the cliff, not less. When you try not to notice something, you've now assigned part of your brain to monitor that thing, ensuring that it stays at the forefront of your awareness, rather than naturally receding to background. Like trying to push a beach ball under the water—as soon as you let go, it's going to come flying right back in your face!

This doesn't necessarily mean that awareness cannot ever change; it just means that we don't do it directly. As someone who worries, you've responded to your awareness in such a way that your brain is now trained to track and pay attention to cues that might not be helpful for you. The worrier notices a what-if thought and assumes that it warrants attention. Instead, we want to allow this symphony of perceptual input to float right by, leaving the useless data unexamined. This requires a command of the next mental process we'll talk about—attention.

Attention

If awareness is about how your brain gathers information about the world, then attention is about how your brain attempts to process that information effectively. You can sort through only so much at one time. If you were to try to compute every last bit of this information at once, you'd be overloaded. So, your brain has a handy feature of being able to shine a spotlight on a smaller selection of data. This is *attention*. It's directing your focus to a more manageable subset of information, usually based on what your brain believes to be most relevant or important at the moment. It's an effort to triage the information that's coming in, prioritizing the data that's useful and discarding the data that's not. If you're sitting in math class, the awareness of extraneous information—what you'll have for lunch that day, what you learned last period about the War of 1812, the feeling of your sock being bunched up—is irrelevant. As long as you continue directing your attention to math class, the awareness of this tangential information will naturally fade out of your awareness on its own.

Attention is within your control. It's not perfect, and you may not always be able to control it with precision or consistency, but you do at least have some say in where you put your focus. If I go to a sports bar to watch the Red Sox and notice that they have twenty TVs with twenty different games on, I can choose to direct my attention to the Red Sox. My attention may get pulled away—maybe I hear an excited announcer calling a homerun in another game—but I can redirect my focus back to my game. My ability to do this depends on a lot of things:

- Is this game *important*? Is it Game 7 of the World Series? Or were the Sox eliminated from playoff contention long ago and this game means nothing?

- Is it *exciting*? Is it bases loaded, full count, bottom of the ninth? Or a routine ground ball in the second inning?

- How am I *feeling*? Am I well rested or tired? Well nourished or hungry? Was I already anxious going into this experience or feeling calm?

- And what about those *distractions*? Are the other TVs huge and loud? Are those other games exciting? Is everyone in the bar paying attention to a different game?

- What's my *mindset* going into this? Did I tell myself that this game would be worth watching only if I could pay full attention the whole time? Do I believe that I *should* be able to pay perfect attention?

Sometimes our brains naturally pay attention to the most relevant things; we can do this effortlessly, intuitively. It can be experienced as an automatic process, requiring no conscious effort at all. Our minds seamlessly shift attention from one thing to another, shining the spotlight precisely where we want it. At other times, the situation is going to demand that we get a bit more deliberate. Our minds are not always firing on all cylinders; they don't perfectly anticipate what we need from them. They can get distracted and make errors in calculating our attention priorities.

I attended college in Vermont and remember how my brain would automatically start to pay more attention when I needed to drive to class in the snow. I'd tune out the distractions, my focus zeroed in on the upcoming turn, the next stop sign, the feeling of my tires' grip on the road. I'd notice the texture of the snow—where it was fluffy and unplowed, where it looked slick or icy. I was instinctively focused and alert.

But my brain was not quite as helpful when I needed to make the three-hour drive back to my parents' house in Massachusetts. It was not uncommon that I'd have to pull over to rest, noticing that my eyes were getting heavy and I was starting to feel tired. Even though I was in far more danger going seventy-five on the highway than I was bopping around the side streets of Burlington in the snow, my brain couldn't quite keep engaged. It was monotonous, routine. I'd roll down the windows to feel the cold, turn up the music to keep alert, or call a friend to stay awake. I was always frustrated that my brain couldn't respond to this longer drive with more focus, that it couldn't triage in the way that I needed it to. My brain stopped paying attention organically and I had to step in, implementing more intentional strategies to keep my focus where I wanted it.

This is often the case with anxiety. Our brains are doing their best to triage—attention gets diverted to what our brains believe to be important and relevant, but unfortunately our brains are fallible. They don't always get it right. Our brains are naturally drawn to the very things that provoke or worsen our anxiety. This is one of the things that make attention tricky—we have some ability to direct our attention, but it's not complete control. I can't say, "Pay attention to the Red Sox," and then have my focus remain solely and permanently on the Red Sox. Instead, I can make efforts to direct my attention to the game, but I'll simultaneously have to contend with the other factors swirling around that may be working against me, pulling me away from my intended goal.

Engagement

Engagement is the most active of these mental processes. If awareness is noticing a thought and attention is shining a spotlight on it, engagement is picking up that thought to examine it. Crucially, engagement involves interaction. For instance, if you're engaging with uncertainty, you're not just noticing or focusing on uncertainty, but trying to resolve it. Or with anxiety, it's not just recognizing anxiety, but trying to make it go away. In essence, this is worrying. It's engaging with a worry thought, whether by ruminating, analysis, mental review, or thought suppression. It's saying, *I want to stop being aware of this, so I'm going to try to resolve it or push it out of my awareness.*

Engagement is volitional. It's you making a choice to solve a problem. When you cross over from "I'm feeling worry" to "I am worrying," you've now become an active participant.

Awareness, Attention, and Engagement Walk into a Bar...

So now we have all of our ingredients. You know the elements at play. The next step is to figure out how to tinker with these basic ingredients so that you are no longer perpetuating worry and the anxiety cycle.

Let's play a game. We've reviewed three mental processes (awareness, attention, and engagement); now, your assignment is to choose a way to interact with each of these processes. Your options: Control, resist, and allow. You get to assign one action to each mental process. I'll start you off by showing you what happens when you worry:

Awareness → Resist

Attention → Control

Engagement → Allow

When you arrange things in this way, you're attempting to block out (resist) the uncomfortable bits of your awareness, and attempting to restrict your experience by trying to force the unwanted thoughts out of your attention or by allowing yourself to engage with the thoughts. Instead, what if we tried this:

Awareness → Allow

Attention → Control

Engagement → Resist

Now we're allowing for awareness, opening ourselves to all thoughts. We're exercising control over attention—directing our attention to what's important while being open to awareness, as opposed to directing our attention away from thoughts to control or limit them. In other words, I can watch the Red Sox game while noticing and acknowledging the other things happening around me, without attempting to make any of it go away. I'll gently redirect my focus back to the game when it gets pulled away. This allows me to resist engagement with worry thoughts.

Master Worrying by Treating It like a Behavior

You may have noticed that these concepts of awareness, attention, and engagement map onto the steps of the anxiety cycle we covered in chapter 2. Like the initial thought or trigger that sets off the anxiety cycle, awareness is uncontrollable. It's merely a byproduct of attention and engagement. If, instead of attempting to subdue your awareness, you direct your energy toward the components that you do control—attention and engagement—you'll be able to subvert this cycle and dismantle it. Luckily for us, there's already a treatment model built for this problem; we just need to get clear about how to apply it to worrying.

What Is Exposure and Response Prevention?

Exposure and response prevention (ERP) is a treatment for OCD that involves systematically confronting fears (exposure) while eliminating the compulsions and safety behaviors that interfere with learning (response prevention). Though this treatment is designed for OCD, the principles can also be applied to anxiety and worry more broadly—since all anxiety, in one way or another, is perpetuated by the same cycle of reinforcement. You can begin to manage your anxiety more effectively by exploiting the weakness in the anxiety cycle and discontinuing the reinforcement that keeps it going.

Theoretically, if you're not in immediate danger, your brain should take note, adjust, and stop setting off its emergency system. If it's not doing this—if you continue to be anxious even in the absence of an immediate threat—something is confusing your brain. Something is going on that is preventing your brain from getting the information that it needs to make a correction.

Most folks with OCD and anxiety have plenty of exposure opportunities—they move through their day, getting triggered by one thing or another. But they don't capitalize on the value of that exposure because they're doing compulsions. When you avoid or engage with unwanted thoughts, your brain is learning that this process is helping you to avoid danger. If you instead opt to allow worry to be present without attempting to limit or change the experience, your brain just might be able to learn that these thoughts don't pose a threat.

Think back to our caveman example in chapter 2—remember the guy who couldn't tell the difference between a bear and a sheep? If he runs back to his cave every time he sees a sheep, he'll never learn to discriminate between bears and sheep. That kind of avoidance comes at a steep opportunity cost. He deprives himself of the chance to gather new information and learn. But there's also another way that he can miss the memo about sheep: if he approaches the sheep, but is wearing full body armor and carrying an axe, he's still going to interfere with learning that a sheep is nothing to be afraid of in reality. He'll walk away believing that his extra precautions were necessary and that they were responsible for his safety.

The same principles apply to our anxious thoughts and whether we choose to feed them with compulsive engagement or avoidance. This is why we need good response prevention. By removing all the qualifiers and conditions, you allow your brain an unfiltered glimpse at the threat that it's facing and allow it to come to a more accurate conclusion about danger. With no confounding variables to muddy the equation, your brain can finally learn what it needs to learn.

Now, you might be asking yourself, *If I can recognize that my fear is irrational or disproportionate, shouldn't that be enough to help my brain to correct course?* Oh, I wish that were the case. But unfortunately, logic and reason can only get you so far. Our fears are rarely rational. If they were, most people who come to my office would be seeking help for their fear of heart disease. After all, that's the thing most likely to kill us. But that's a pretty rare occurrence in my office. People seek help for their fear of public speaking, or flying, or leaving their house unlocked, all of which are quite unlikely to kill you. The things that scare us are usually not the things that pose an actual threat.

Let's consider flying for a moment. You've probably heard the same statistical conclusion that I have: planes are safer than cars. In fact, you're more likely to die on the way to the airport than on the actual plane. So why is it that when the plane hits a patch of turbulence, my stomach jumps into my chest and I grip my armrests? Why do I feel scared when I know that I'm safe? The answer can be found in the flight attendants. What do they do when the plane hits a patch of turbulence? They carry on. They keep handing out their drinks and peanuts, completely apathetic, uninterested. Do they *intellectually* know something that we don't know? Probably not. But they *experientially* know something that we don't. They ride on planes every day. Their knowledge that turbulence is normal is not just academic; the flight attendants have learned it by living and doing. They've seen firsthand that turbulence comes and goes and that they are perfectly capable of carrying on without paying heed to the bumps. It's not that they know more than the rest of us—it's that they've built the requisite learning to experience the situation differently.

This reflects a reality that is pivotal to ERP: experiential learning is key. When I was a kid, I used to love this game called *The Legend of Zelda* on the original Nintendo. All the other game cartridges were a dull grey;

this one was shiny gold. It was glorious. Each level had a boss that you would need to defeat, but the trick was figuring out how to do it. If you didn't find the right strategy, your efforts would all be in vain. To defeat the giant one-eyed spider, for instance, you had to make sure that you shot your arrow only when its eye was open; otherwise, your arrows were useless. To defeat the triceratops, you had to make sure you put your bomb directly in its path; otherwise, it wouldn't eat the bomb and the explosion would do no harm.

When you want to defeat anxiety and worry, you have to strategically plan your intervention. You can't just toss your weapons around willy-nilly; you have to understand what strategy actually has the potential to be effective. Logic and reasoning are like arrows shot at the spider while its eye is closed, bombs placed next to rather than in front of the triceratops. They just won't get the job done. If you want to access your brain's fear system, experiential learning is the way to get through.

What Happens When You Do ERP?

When you're exposed to the same trigger over and over again, what typically results is *habituation*; eventually, the amount of distress that you experience will decrease. You can think of it like jumping into a cold pool in the summer—the water will feel cold at first, but if you stay in the water, it will eventually start to feel warmer. The temperature of the water doesn't change, of course, but you start to experience it differently. If, however, you jump right back out after feeling the cold, you'll never get to have that experience. All you'll feel is cold. ERP works in the same way—if you stay in the exposure, eventually the distress will start to decrease. It will go down over time, even if you do nothing about it. Conversely, if you disrupt that process—by avoidance, compulsion, or Distraction—you'll never get to experience habituation.

When it comes to ERP, habituation is a lovely outcome. And I certainly don't begrudge anyone the desire to have their distress reduced. It's also not necessarily the goal. In fact, there are actually a few problems with it:

- Habituation doesn't always happen reliably. Everyone's brain is a little different. For example, some emotions, like fear, tend to respond a bit more predictably than others, like disgust (McKay 2006).

- Those who habituate more don't necessarily fair better in treatment. Studies have shown that greater habituation at the end of treatment does not always predict better treatment outcomes (Baker et al. 2010). That is, some people habituate, but don't necessarily improve; others improve without much habituation.

- Habituation can be antithetical to the goal of exposure. Ideally when you're doing ERP, you're practicing making yourself open to whatever emotional experience shows up. This means that you're not going into it saying, "I hope my anxiety goes down," but rather, "I'm going to be willing to allow anxiety to come and go without trying to change it."

Habituation may be a nice byproduct, but it's not the explicit goal of ERP.

What we're more interested in during ERP is *learning*. Exposure is an opportunity to teach your brain something new. Your brain has stumbled into certain expectations about how things are going to go and what kinds of things you need to do to keep yourself safe. Exposure allows an opportunity to adjust those expectations. When it comes to worry, your brain has made a few fundamental assumptions that we're looking to challenge:

- Thoughts are dangerous and warrant attention.

- By examining thoughts (engagement), I can eliminate danger.

- I'm not capable of being uncertain.

- I'm not capable of being distressed.

Instead, we want to build opportunities to learn that:

- Thoughts are not dangerous and don't necessarily warrant attention.

- I do not need to examine every thought that arises to be safe.

- I am capable of allowing uncertainty without resolving it.

- I am capable of feeling distress without attempting to make it go away.

You see, your brain's just gotten a bit confused. It needs to have a corrective experience and to learn something new. You're the one in charge of managing these experiences. You're the concierge, arranging for the circumstances that will maximize the learning possibilities to create a new relationship to your thoughts. You don't need to grip your seat during turbulence. And you don't need to wrestle every thought into submission.

How Do You Apply Response Prevention to a Mental Behavior?

This approach usually feels pretty intuitive when it comes to external, physical behaviors, but people often get stuck when they need to tailor it to a mental behavior. You'll remember that the anxiety cycle can be perpetuated by two types of responses: efforts to reduce anxiety (worrying, compulsion) and efforts to prevent anxiety (avoidance). To stop the wheel and break free of the cycle, we'll need to remove the parts that keep it going. Let's take a look at how these behavioral principles are applied to mental processes.

Mental Avoidance

Physical avoidance is usually straightforward enough. If you have a phobia of dogs or planes, you avoid going near dogs or planes. If you are worried about dirt or germs, you might avoid going to public places or use barriers like gloves or shirt sleeves to prevent yourself from feeling contaminated. If you're worried about finances, you might avoid checking your bank statement so that you don't trigger an onslaught of worrying. These are all methods of preventing anxiety. By exerting control over your circumstances, you can attempt to limit your triggers. As you know, this strategy is shortsighted in that it will ultimately make your anxiety worse, not better. These behaviors might limit anxiety triggers temporarily, but in doing so, they power the anxiety cycle and strengthen your brain's association between the trigger (dogs, planes, germs, finances) and danger.

But what does avoidance look like when it's not a tangible, external behavior? Some triggers happen right inside your own head. Mental avoidance is when you attempt to limit these internal triggers, usually by thought suppression or Distraction. These behaviors are meant to target and snuff out awareness. They're efforts to try to shrink down your perception, narrowing the scope of your viewfinder so that you are no longer conscious of the unwanted experiences.

If we think back to our sports bar metaphor, thought suppression would probably mean attempting to turn off all the other TVs so that I was blissfully unaware that any other games were on. Distraction would probably mean turning the volume up as loud as possible on the Sox game or maybe sitting two feet from the screen so that I wasn't as aware of the other unwanted TVs.

The trouble here is that in the sports bar of your mind, the TVs can't be turned off—remember, you don't control awareness directly. And every time you ask the bartender (your brain) to turn down the volume on the other TVs, they misunderstand and do the exact opposite. They turn them all up, until they're blaring and all-consuming and it feels like you'll never be able to focus on your game ever again. No, thought suppression isn't the way to go.

And Distraction won't be much help either. You could park yourself right in front of the TV, put in earplugs, and refuse to talk to anyone. But what kind of life is that? Is that how you'll need to watch every game? Is it really in line with the kind of experience you want to have? The kind of person you want to be? And what happens when eventually earplugs are insufficient and you need step it up to noise-canceling headphones? Or watch the game alone, at home, in utter silence lest someone interfere and disrupt your focus? No, chances are your Distraction will also come at a cost, gradually diminishing your ability to coexist with the things competing for your attention.

Mental Compulsions (a.k.a. Worrying)

Most folks know the telltale signs of a compulsion. A compulsive behavior is excessive, repetitive, and disproportionate. It's when someone washes their hands over and over again, even though they didn't touch anything dangerous. It's the person going back to check the locks on their door, even though they're *pretty sure* they locked it. While behaviors like these are definitely red flags, these elements alone don't make a compulsion. The important unseen ingredient is function: compulsions are behaviors intended to *prevent or reduce distress*.

Let's use contamination obsessions as an example. If you're concerned that you might get sick, you can try to prevent that outcome in lots of physical ways:

- Avoiding touching "dirty" surfaces

- Washing your hands

- Cleaning

- Quarantining "clean" and "dirty" items

- Asking others for reassurance

- Requiring others to follow your sanitation rules

While these observable, physical behaviors often get the bulk of our clinical attention, there are many compulsive behaviors that happen behind the closed doors of your mind:

- Mentally tracking which items have become contaminated

- Replaying your actions to ensure that you didn't do something risky

- Calculating the likelihood that you'll get sick

- Mentally gauging whether you feel sick

- Planning for how you'll respond if you get sick

Like physical compulsions, mental compulsions also functionally reinforce OCD and anxiety. They send your brain the message that there is a threat by treating doubt and uncertainty like they're dangerous. They ensure that your brain will continue to track and pay attention to these triggers, believing your mental efforts to be essential to your survival.

Take a moment to consider how you tend to respond to doubts and worries in your life. How much mental energy is spent trying to eliminate doubt? How might you be reinforcing your worry and anxiety with your mental habits? Grab a pen and paper and try the following exercise:

1. Write down a current or recent worry.

2. In what ways did you attempt to mentally avoid? Did you try to push thoughts out of your awareness? Did you attempt to limit your exposure to potential triggers? Did you Distract yourself to stop thinking about it? Jot down the things you did to try to prevent the experience of worry.

3. What brand of worrying did you use (e.g., mental review, analysis, reassurance, etc.)? Did you keep trying to figure it out even though a definitive answer couldn't be found? Did you run mental simulations of unlikely scenarios? Were you hypervigilant or tracking potential indicators of danger? Identify the responses that could be maintaining your worry habit.

4. What do you think your brain learned from these mental gymnastics? Given these responses, do you think your brain will be more likely or less likely to assess this worry as a threat in the future?

So How Do You Resist Mental Avoidance and Mental Compulsions?

You'll need to tailor your approach to effectively address each one of these mental processes: awareness, attention, and engagement. Like the bosses in *The Legend of Zelda*, each one has a weakness, a point of attack. Here's the short version: separate worry from worrying. Allow awareness of the initial unwanted thought, but use your attention such that you don't lapse into a process of avoidance, Distraction, or engagement. And rather than training your attention on the offending thought, allow the thought to exist within your awareness while redirecting your attention back to what matters. In this way, you'll starve your anxiety of what's keeping it going and give your brain new opportunities to learn how to operate more effectively. In the next chapter, we'll provide concrete tools you can practice to help you disrupt the cycle of anxiety by disengaging from worrying.

CHAPTER EIGHT

Non-Engagement Strategies

In the final count, it takes less effort, even less
courage, to go forward with true acceptance than to
go forward fighting grimly.

—Claire Weekes

As you know by now, you're not going to "just stop" worrying. You recognize that worrying is unhelpful and want to be able to let it go, but when the rubber hits the road, you can't just channel your inner "chill" and forget about it. Well, here's the part that no one likes to hear: if you want to get better at this, you're going to have to practice. Nothing in this book will make all of your troubles go away, but by building and practicing these skills, you can ensure that these uncomfortable experiences don't take up any more space than they need to.

Our goal is to have worry, without worrying; allow for awareness, without getting stuck struggling with it. When you're trying to break a habit and create a new one, it's generally easier to *do something* than to *not do something*. Rather than telling my kid, "Don't be mean to your sister," it will work better if I say, "Maybe you could try talking to your sister like *this*." You know by now that your goal is to stop worrying, but you're going to need some things to do instead.

Let's review our blueprint from chapter 7:

Awareness → Allow

Attention → Change

Engagement → Resist

Non-engagement is both the process and the outcome. When you accept your internal experience and direct your attention where you'd like it (rather than immediately shining your attention spotlight on doubt), you will stop perpetuating the anxiety cycle. This chapter is going to provide tools for both acceptance and change, learning to allow and embrace uncertainty, while also strengthening your ability to direct your attention so that you're not at the mercy of your thoughts.

Awareness Is the MacGuffin

You're probably familiar with *not* solving problems. In fact, right now, as you read this, there are millions of problems that you're leaving unsolved: What's the meaning of life? What's the square root of 7,831? What's the best route to get to the airport? Where's Amelia Earhart? Whatever happened to that sock that went into the laundry and never returned?

Sometimes these questions have answers, sometimes they don't. Sometimes the answers are important or relevant, sometimes they're not. It's up to us to determine when our efforts to solve a problem are useful and when we'd be better off allowing the mystery of the lost sock to go unsolved.

In film and literature, there is a concept called the "MacGuffin." A MacGuffin is a narrative device that propels the characters into action, while remaining somewhat tangential or irrelevant to the story itself. It's the mysterious briefcase in *Pulp Fiction*, the peed-on rug in *The Big Lebowski*, the stolen Death Star plans in *Star Wars*. These items push the characters into action, driving the plot forward toward a resolution. Without the MacGuffin to set things into motion, the characters would just continue on, unperturbed, with no reason to deviate from their ordinary lives. If Darth Vader never goes looking for the plans at the beginning of *Star Wars*, then Luke doesn't cross paths with the droids, he never leaves his uncle's farm to find Ben, and there's no space adventure; if The Dude just says, "Whatever, man," about his peed-on rug, he doesn't meet the millionaire Lebowski, and there's no movie.

Awareness of a problem or doubt is the MacGuffin of your struggle with anxiety. Whatever internal experiences show up in our minds—thoughts, feelings, urges, sensations—they are what they are. Your awareness of them in your mind is like the MacGuffin showing up in a movie. Just as the MacGuffin sets things into motion, awareness can spur you into action. A movie plot happens when its characters chase the MacGuffin, and worrying happens when you chase awareness of problems or doubt by engaging with worry thoughts. Awareness is the hook that propels the whole cycle of worrying—a saga that rarely ends in a tidy resolution.

But you don't have to chase the MacGuffin. You don't have to detour from your everyday life. You don't have to engage with the thoughts or make anxiety go away, and you don't need resolution. When that MacGuffin shows up, goading you into action, you're better off sitting it out. Your mission is to eliminate the movie by not chasing the MacGuffin, tempting as it may be.

Practice Acceptance by Writing

If the goal is not to heroically vanquish uncertainty, then instead we're shooting to accept (and even embrace) uncertainty. One tool that can help in your quest for acceptance is writing. *Coping scripts* (also called *response prevention scripts*) are a technique to help you to stay on message, to bring you back to the spirit of your mission in moments when you feel pulled to go on that MacGuffin-chasing quest. The goal is to write a short narrative to remind yourself of what you're trying to do. It's to acknowledge the inevitability of uncertainty, while simultaneously giving yourself a pep talk. When anxiety shows up and thoughts get loud, it becomes harder to conjure up what your therapist said in your last session; you can lose sight of what you're supposed to do, becoming overwhelmed by the power of your internal experience. The goal is to make it as easy as possible to correct course; so rather than hoping that you'll have the wherewithal to remember these things in the moment, you can remove that barrier by preparing ahead of time. If you have a coping script ready to go, you can simply refer to it in the moment, sending a message from non-anxious you to the current anxious you who's stuck in it.

Guidelines for Crafting Your Coping Script

It can be broad or specific. You can save yourself some time and energy by creating a coping script that is general enough that it could apply to any worry that may arise. Alternatively, if you find that a particular worry seems to be more prevalent than others, it may be worthwhile to ditch the one-size-fits-all approach and tailor your script more to your specific worry. This may be especially salient for folks with OCD, who may find that their worry tends to be connected to one specific obsession.

Don't shy away from the hard stuff. This is not necessarily a feel-good exercise. The goal is not to accept uncertainty so that the bad feelings will go away; it's to accept it because resisting and struggling with reality is getting you nowhere. You don't need sugarcoating; you don't need avoidance. You are capable of experiencing the full weight of reality, without needing anything to obfuscate it. If the hard truth is that you can't ever have certainty, then come right out and say it.

Keep it fresh. We all get bored with the same thing over and over again. You'll eventually tune out that sticky note on your desk or the recurring reminder on your phone. If you really want these kinds of things to stick, you'll benefit from having some novelty. Change the wording, rewrite it occasionally, add new motivators, subtract old ones.

Include your go-to nuggets of wisdom. You've probably stumbled across a few favorite tidbits of information—an example or metaphor that stuck with you, a quote or experience that solidified your resolve to get better.

These kinds of reminders are great to include in a coping script. It's a pep-talk built just for you, incorporating your "greatest hits" of motivation.

Remember what worry has cost you. In the moment, worrying can seem harmless. But remember, it does its damage cumulatively. In any given moment, worrying might not cost you much, but it compounds. Like smoking cigarettes, it's easy to rationalize that one cigarette won't kill you, but this approach ignores the true cost—the long-term, repetition of this behavior can take a toll. How much time has been spent looking for an answer that never arrived? Or preparing for an unlikely event, which never came to fruition? How has your worry impacted your relationships? Or your job? Don't be afraid to include these kinds of reminders in your script.

Keep it relatively short. I usually recommend less than a page, maybe two to three paragraphs. You don't want to have to read a novel every time you're trying to get yourself back on track.

Use first-person language. Coping scripts usually work best if you use "I" language. It tends to feel more real and authentic for most people. Alternatively, if you suspect that writing to yourself using "you" instead would be more helpful, then by all means give it a shot. There's always room to get flexible and find what works for you.

Don't reassure yourself with content. A coping script may be sort of a pep talk, but not the kind that pretends that everything will be okay. The future is uncertain and you are capable of existing in a world where you can't nail it all down. Don't sell yourself short by offering false platitudes of certainty. If you *are* using specific content, you want to stay away from sentiments that attempt to convince you that the unwanted outcomes will not happen (or even that they're unlikely).

Here are two examples of coping scripts—the first is more general and the second uses a specific worry (a fear of being responsible for harming others):

Example 1 (General)

The kind of person I want to be is confident. Assured in my decisions. Trusting of myself. I want to be in control of my life, not controlled by my worries. And as much as it pains me to admit it, I can't be that person unless I learn to accept uncertainty.

I've spent countless hours "trying to figure it out." Hours and hours of my life spent in the pursuit of something that is never coming. My brain has promised me certainty, but that's a lie. It's convinced me that I'll have peace when I can finally get an answer, but I'm sick and tired of its unfulfilled promises. I know now that the only way I get freedom is to take it for myself. I don't need certainty. I can withstand anxiety. These things won't control me anymore.

It's going to be uncomfortable, but I can handle that. I know that the best thing that I can do for myself is to allow discomfort. The best gift I can give to future-me is to start that learning now, to build the habits, piece by piece, so that future-me knows how to be uncertain. So here I go! I'm going to let these thoughts and these feelings come along for the ride. I won't fight them anymore. They won't take any more of my time.

Example 2 (Specific)

My brain keeps telling me that the stove might be on. It really wants me to be sure, even though it's only a faint possibility. It wants me to check, to pour over the fragments of my memory to try to find clarity. It reminds me of how awful it would be if the house burned down and I was responsible. It conjures up image after terrible image of the fiery aftermath.

It all feels so powerful, but I've been down this road before. I know that these scary ideas are the bait that tricks me into feeding the anxiety cycle. I know that if I want any kind of life for myself, I'm going to have to take some risks. These thoughts are scary, but thoughts are just thoughts. I don't need to respond to imagined scenarios like they're my reality. So I'll move on. The doubt will gradually fade, like it always does. It'll recede once again to the background, always a possibility, but not an urgent demand.

I've checked that stove a thousand times. Repeated checking has never brought me peace; it's never guaranteed the safety of my family. It's taken a lot from me, giving me next to nothing in return and keeping me stuck. I know now that the way I express care for my family is by breaking free. When I'm present—not stuck in my head, not constantly seeking reassurance—that's when I truly connect with the people around me; that's how I can show my love for them. I'm going to feel anxious for a bit. And these thoughts might keep chirping at me for a while. But I'm committed to allowing them to be there without sinking into a mental argument with myself. I want to spend more time in my life and less time in my head.

Implementing Your Coping Script

Once you've written your coping script, it's now ready to use! When you're experiencing anxiety or worry and you start to feel a pull to engage—to make the anxiety go away, to resolve the doubt—go to your coping script. Read it and try your best to really connect with the sentiment. The goal is to get yourself to a place where you're no longer immersed in the thoughts, but instead, you're observing them and making a conscious choice not to engage. You're accepting that the mystery of the lost sock may never be solved and committing yourself to not finding it.

A couple of quick troubleshooting tips:

- **Don't be a robot.** If you find yourself reading your script in a detached, rote kind of way, pause for moment. If you just read it over and over again, you're likely to become more disconnected, not less. So try taking a quick break—take a few mindful breaths, listen to a song—then come back to it.

- **Don't turn your script into a compulsion.** Remember, these scripts are also sometimes called response prevention scripts, and that's because their function is to aid in resisting compulsions (or worrying). Your script is not meant to make your anxiety go away; it's meant to be a tool to help you to resist worrying and move on. Sure, if you do that, chances are good that your anxiety will go down, but that is not the explicit goal. The more you try not to be anxious, the more anxious you'll be. So don't forget: you're doing this to accept your internal experience, not change it.

- **Acceptance of worry, not worrying.** By this point, you could probably put it on a bumper sticker: you have to accept your thoughts and feelings, not fight them. But please keep in mind a really important distinction—we're talking about accepting the initial, unwanted thought that just shows up in your head, the awareness of doubt. We're not saying that you should accept rumination. Rumination is an active, volitional process, and you can absolutely choose not to do that. Accept the initial thought, but decline the invitation to examine it. Allow the uncomfortable feeling, but resist the urge to make it go away.

Flex Your Attention Muscle

As we discussed in the previous chapter, attention is a mechanism used by your brain to narrow its focus, preventing overload by selecting only the most relevant information. There are lots of different criteria for determining what rises to the top of our attention priority list, but the thing best suited to commandeering our attention is danger. To survive, we need a certain amount of vigilance to the threats around us.

In my backyard, I tend to get a lot of rabbits. They happily munch on the grass (and whatever vegetables I was naïve enough to plant), lounging peacefully and nibbling away to their hearts' content. That is, until we let our dog out. The rabbits used to sprint through the fence as soon as they saw the dog come out the door, but now they seem to have figured out that our dog is no match for them. She'll give chase, but she's old and really doesn't stand a chance. So now they just hunker down. They'll freeze, hoping to avoid being detected, but you can see their ears moving around, tracking our dog, waiting for the moment when the dog gets too close. They're not fighting or fleeing—just watching. Paying attention.

This aspect of attention is adaptive if you're a little bunny evading predators. Unfortunately, if you channel your attention in situations where there is no actual threat, you may find that this mechanism begins to work against rather than for you. As long as you keep paying attention to the things that trigger you, you'll remain stuck in the anxiety feedback loop, showing your brain that your vigilance was necessary to keep you safe. To discontinue that cycle of reinforcement, you'll need to stop paying attention.

Now let's be clear: Shifting your attention is not the same as Distraction. Distraction is about limiting your awareness; it pushes away the uncomfortable internal experiences. It's a band-aid, a concession that you make when you haven't yet built the skills to mindfully focus your attention. Distraction is like putting on horse-blinders—artificially blocking out the richness and texture of life, preferring instead to navigate the world by making it as small and trigger-free as possible. It sends your brain the message, *You're not capable of handling this thought or this feeling. To be okay, you have to do something to make it go away.*

Shifting your attention is something different. Nothing needs to be pushed out of your awareness. You can acknowledge the presence of a thought. You can make space for it, without attending to it. Thoughts, the awareness of thoughts—these things cannot hurt you. You don't need to handle them with kid gloves. You can allow them to be, coming and going as they please. Pay them no mind. You don't have to push them away, nor do you need to spend your time wrestling with them. You can hold these things in your awareness while directing your attention elsewhere.

Here are some exercises you can try to build your attention muscle.

The Sock-Penny Game

What do you do when you have a mosquito bite? Do you try not to scratch it? Cover it up? Put anti-itch cream on it? Have you ever wondered why you only notice the itchiness of your mosquito bite for part of your day? It's not a constant. Even the biggest, itchiest mosquito bite will fade out of your awareness for periods throughout the day. And then you'll remember—maybe you graze it with your hand or your clothing rubs against it. The awareness of it will come roaring right back, front and center. And if you scratch it? Oooh boy. Now it's really itching. But again, your brain will eventually tune it out. You'll get absorbed into the demands of your day, forgetting all about it until inevitably something brings it back to your awareness again. You'll go through this process over and over and over again. The trick is that you can't engage with it (scratching) and you can't *try* not to notice it (because that will just keep it at the forefront). Instead, you'll need to relinquish control. Truly, authentically, allow yourself to move on and get back to living life, allowing your awareness of the mosquito bite to recede on its own rather than pushing it away. If you treat it like it's irrelevant, your brain will follow suit. Worry works in the same way—it will come in and out of your awareness, periodically screaming loudly, but fading as you refocus on life.

While I'm not quite sadistic enough to have my clients seek out mosquitoes to practice, I do have them play The Sock-Penny Game. The "game" part is really a misnomer. Let's call it an experiment. Your job is to put a penny in your sock. That's it! Just annoying enough to grab your attention, but subtle enough that your awareness will fade if you let it. If the penny is too difficult, you can start with a cotton ball and work your way up. The goal is *not* to not notice the penny; it's to not *try* to not notice the penny. That's a mouthful. Let's put that another way: Clients often come to my office after having played the sock-penny game and are ecstatic when they can report, "I barely noticed it by the end!" And I'll usually say something like, "That's cool. But is noticing it bad? Isn't our goal to stop caring if we notice it and just carry on?" We're practicing directing our attention toward what we want, rather than away from what we don't want. It's a subtle difference, but an important one. We're shooting for a peaceful coexistence, a world in which we expand to make space for uncomfortable experiences.

If you want to really lean into this one, you can spice it up by adding some reminders. Put a sticky note on your computer screen that reads "sock penny." Set a reminder on your phone—"Don't forget about the penny!" Sprinkle your desktop with socks. Or pennies. Or both! Get into the spirit of this—it's not about pushing the experience out of your awareness; it's about forging a new relationship to awareness by noticing, and then consistently redirecting your focus back to your life.

You may be asking yourself: *What on earth do sock pennies have to do with worrying?* Reasonable question. First, it's not really about sock pennies. The sock pennies are just an innocuous stand-in for worries. They're stripped of content (unless you happen to have had a traumatic sock-penny experience in your formative years). But they could be anything. You could have sticky notes on your computer screen that read, "Don't forget about your massive financial debt!" or a reminder on your phone that says, "What if you forgot to lock the front door?!" I know it sounds silly, or maybe even scary, but if you can be aware of discomfort without content, you can do it with content. If you can disengage from a neutral thought, you can also disengage from one that's more charged. These are all just thoughts—some have accompanying feelings—others don't. You don't have an obligation to pay attention to any of them, regardless of content.

The second reason we do this is because learning to disengage is a skill. That's why you can't just snap your fingers and stop worrying. You have to actually learn, practice, and develop skills so that you're no longer stuck in it. So practice this! It could be a sock penny. Or a back-pocket marble. A feather in your shirtsleeve. Or a thought about your finances while you're trying to work. Doesn't matter. Get really good at noticing and pivoting back to what matters. Learn to build your attention muscle by having your focus pulled away, then bringing it back to the task at hand.

Burpees for Your Brain

Attention shifting is an important part of mastering worrying. Once you become aware of your worry, you can't stop at noticing or acknowledging—you have to actively disengage and refocus your attention on the present moment. This may seem hard now, but you can get better at it—you just have to practice!

When I first learned to play guitar, I learned a few basic chords—D, G, and C. Once I got a feel for the chords, the next step was to practice moving back and forth between them. To make these discrete sounds into a song, I had to master the seamless transition between the chords. This is how we're going to approach attention—it's not enough to get really good at focusing; you're going to need to practice shifting between various iterations of paying attention. Here are the chords for your attention practice:

Open Awareness: Allow your attention to drift. Your awareness is broad, and if you unfocus your mind, you can allow your attention to land on whatever pulls it. Let it drift, uncontrolled, meandering from one thing to another without any efforts to siphon your attention into anything in particular. This is not engagement; it's not intentional. It's letting the flow of your awareness exist without hindrance, without being channeled in any intentional direction. Let yourself be pulled, rather than pushing.

Focused Attention: Shine the spotlight of your attention directly onto various aspects of your awareness. Notice the sounds of the birds outside or traffic in the distance. The clock ticking in the background. Feel the aches in your body, the texture of your seat. Notice the faint taste of your morning coffee in your mouth, the smell of the air around you. Acknowledge the thoughts that drift into your mind, the feelings that exist when you stop and slow down. Intentionally move the spotlight of your attention to these different stimuli, directing it deliberately from one thing to the next. Don't linger on anything in particular. This is attention speed dating. Direct your attention momentarily to each item, maybe for five to ten seconds, then move on.

Sustained Attention: Now, keep your spotlight on one thing. You'll notice the other elements around you, grabbing your attention, vying to pull you away or suck you into engagement. Notice these things, allowing them to exist in your awareness but without commandeering your attention. Pick something and keep your attention on it, gently bringing yourself back in moments when something else makes a play for your attention. The emphasis is on *gentle*—don't block out the distractions or beat yourself up when you get pulled away. Bring your focus back to your target with slow and steady care.

Next, your job is to pivot. Once you've had some practice with each of these individual exercises, you'll next practice vacillating back and forth between these states of attention. I'd recommend starting with about a minute for each one. If you're struggling, feel free to drop it down to whatever amount of time you feel you can practice consistently. As you practice, you'll be able to hold each one a little bit longer. Move from one to the next and repeat. Like changing chords, the goal is to master these distinct aspects of attention so that you can "play" them as you need to.

Remember, this is about practice. If you do it more, you'll get more benefit. In an ideal world, I'd ask my clients to practice this for about fifteen to twenty minutes each day. I recognize that this kind of practice can be difficult to get into and sustain, so please start with whatever frequency and amount of time is manageable for you. If a few minutes is what you can muster, that's perfectly fine. And remember, don't make this compulsive! It's not a tool to make anxiety go away in moments when you're triggered; it's an exercise to build a skill that is integral to your management of anxiety.

I don't play guitar that much these days. I have a bunch of young kids, work is busy, I just don't fit it in consistently. I still remember all the chords. I could tell you which fret and string each finger should be placed on, but that doesn't mean I'm good at the guitar. The callouses on my fingers are long gone. I'm sure if I picked it up again and got into a more regular practice, a lot of it would come back to me. But I'd have to find time to practice consistently. You probably know where I'm going with this: knowing how to stop worrying and putting in the time to practice the skills to stop worrying are two very different things.

More Ways to Unhook from Thoughts

In this chapter, we deconstructed the ways in which your brain triages information, highlighting awareness, attention, and engagement. We also looked at tools to strengthen your non-engagement skills and navigate this process more effectively.

In the next chapter, we're going to continue building skills to aid in disconnecting from sticky thoughts. Acceptance and commitment therapy (ACT) is a treatment model that can be helpful when re-centering your experience—moving from a life dictated by thoughts and feelings and instead shifting toward one guided by values and meaning. To do this, you'll first need to hone the ability to observe these internal experiences for what they are and then find ways to step out of your thoughts and feelings.

CHAPTER NINE

Defusion from Your Thoughts

I asked myself about the present: how wide it was,
how deep it was, how much of it was mine to keep.

—Kurt Vonnegut, *Slaughterhouse-Five*

Human beings have a complicated relationship with awareness. It's one of the things that separates us from other animals. We don't merely have thoughts, feelings, and instincts; we *know* that we have them. It's this *knowing* that is tricky. Humans have the capacity for meta-awareness— the recognition of our internal mental processes—but we don't access it consistently. We have the capacity to mentally zoom out, harnessing our bird's-eye view of our own experience with great clarity, but we can also get completely lost and immersed in our thoughts and feelings.

We possess a wonderful gift in our ability to hold awareness of our inner life, but we'll need to develop and hone that skill to make the most of it. When we are able to get free from entanglement with our thoughts, we're able to live a life where these internal experiences do not dictate our fate, but they're merely passengers along for the ride. We are capable of being at the helm of our perception, but to access that ability consistently, we all need practice.

The strategies in this book are drawn from several different treatment modalities. There are bits and pieces of cognitive behavioral therapy

(CBT), ACT, MCT, and inference-based cognitive behavioral therapy (IBT). That's a lot of acronyms for one book! One of the reasons I've chosen this particular blend of modalities is that, while they're all different, these approaches also overlap in certain places. Each one incorporates some aspect of noticing your internal experience to cultivate a new perspective—learning to respond from a place where you are no longer lost in that experience, and instead, you become the intentional observer of it. By cultivating awareness of your present-moment experience and separating from it, you can build agency so that you are not entirely at the mercy of your imagination and can respond to these mental experiences in any way you see fit.

This concept is discussed in different ways across modalities—ACT involves a focus on mindfulness and thought defusion. MCT builds the skill of detached mindfulness. IBT targets imaginal absorption by connecting with the here and now. While we can certainly parse through the differences between these concepts, they are ultimately far more alike than different. They each begin with cultivating an awareness of our internal experience (a thought, a feeling, a belief, a reasoning process) and then capitalizing on this moment of perspective and context to move toward a more adaptive response. Each of these modalities, in their own way, recognizes the importance of learning to relate to your inner life differently. Before you can hope to eliminate worrying, you first have to be able to catch and recognize it in the moment.

The goal of this chapter is to help you see your mind's shenanigans for what they are. But before we delve too far into learning defusion skills, let's first get clear on the concepts.

What Is Fusion?

You may be familiar with the term *cognitive fusion*, though there are actually lots of different types of fusion. Like the name implies, fusion is what happens when you get stuck in your internal experience, becoming immersed in your thoughts or feelings. You lose your grasp on your observing mind; thoughts and feelings begin to paint your reality. Fusion is when you struggle to separate from these fleeting mental experiences, instead allowing them to color your perception and dictate your behavior. You're unable to pull yourself away—unable to see your thoughts as merely thoughts, or feelings as the transient emotional surge that they are. You are *fused* with the ephemeral rush of mental abstraction or the temporary flow of emotion, rather than grounded in your own observing perspective. When you're consumed by these private experiences, buried underneath a cloud of thought, the *you* that exists underneath gets lost. But you are not your thoughts or feelings. You are something separate. To unearth you, as a separate entity, you'll first need to defuse.

Let's explore a few common types of fusion.

Thought-Action Fusion

This is when you start to conflate thoughts with actions, and ideas with reality. *If you think it, it will happen. Thinking is as bad as doing.* In thought-action fusion, the line between thought and behavior becomes blurred and the two begin to be treated as if they are equivalent. Individuals with OCD (Shafran, Thordarson, and Rachman 1996) and GAD (Hazlett-Stevens, Zucker, and Craske 2002) have both been found to score higher on measures of thought-action fusion. Thought-action fusion usually manifests in two ways:

Superstitious Superpower

Referred to in the literature as "likelihood thought-action fusion," this aspect of thought-action fusion is kind of like a cosmic jinx. It usually involves the belief that particular thoughts or even the awareness of thoughts may affect an outcome. Sometimes people believe that thinking about something bad will make that bad thing more likely (e.g., *If I think about the dog dying, it will die*); at other times, they may believe that thinking something good will result in a karmic compensatory shift (e.g., *If I think about the dog living a long, happy life, it will die*). Or sometimes, by merely turning your thoughts or energy toward a particular outcome, you've swung the winds of fate in a different direction (e.g., *I noticed that the dog is okay, so now it won't be okay*).

In each of these examples, the thought is given power to sway the outcome. It's not uncommon for people with high levels of thought-action fusion to begin to feel a sense of responsibility for their thoughts and to begin to suppress those thoughts (Thompson-Hollands, Farchione, and Barlow 2013). When it feels like there's a straight line from thought to consequence, or even a more a nebulous cosmic ripple-effect, people often feel an obligation to refrain from thinking bad thoughts to prevent harm. *If I think about the dog dying, I will cause it to die. Therefore, I'm responsible for only thinking good thoughts to protect the dog.* Unfortunately, these efforts to control or suppress thoughts inadvertently reinforce the anxiety cycle and increase worry.

Sometimes thought-action fusion is also perpetuated by the belief that by thinking about something, you are fundamentally changing something about yourself. For example, by thinking a violent thought, you're becoming desensitized and will become more likely to act on it. In case you're wondering, this is generally not how thinking works. We all have intrusive thoughts and these unwanted mental blips do not have any bearing on our actions. One study (Collardeau et al. 2019) even examined this phenomenon in postpartum mothers, looking at the relationship between intrusive thoughts about harm and the connection with real actions of harm—there was no connection. These mothers who were tormented by obsessive thoughts related to harm were no more likely to act on them. While these harm-specific thoughts are most typical of OCD, thought-action fusion is associated with other anxiety disorders as well, including GAD, social anxiety, and panic disorder (Thompson-Hollands, Farchione, and Barlow 2013).

Moral Failing

The other type of thought-action fusion is related to morality and involves a belief that thoughts are good or bad, that there is a moral or ethical component to the thoughts that cycle through our minds. Examples include:

- *Thinking something is just as bad as doing it.*

- *The presence of an upsetting thought means something about me.*

- *I shouldn't be having this thought.*

The misinterpretation of these cognitive experiences is important, as it creates a heightened sense of responsibility and a need for action (Shafran, Thordarson, and Rachman 1996)—*If it's bad to have this thought, then I'm responsible for taking action.* It propels you to attempt to control world events and protect those around you simply by changing your thoughts. From this perspective, it makes sense that you might try to resolve your thoughts or steer them in a particular direction.

But thoughts are not actions. We don't need to control them, prevent them, or suppress them. They won't hurt us or anyone else. A thought is a thought. It's a collection of words or images. A concept. An abstraction. It's not reality, it's a mental representation of reality. Should we lock up Stephen King for all of the scary thoughts he's had? Which ring of hell should Dante reside in for having conjured up all those awful things in *Inferno*? Luckily, our ability to mentally evoke upsetting ideas is not cause for concern.

Let's imagine that you go to an art museum. You're meandering along and you stumble upon a painting of...you. But this isn't any old portrait. What if it shows you committing violence? What if the title reads *Portrait of a Murderer*? Would that make you a murderer? Would you conclude that you are a bad person simply because the painting says so? What if it portrays you as a clown? Or an accountant? These are concepts. Like all ideas, they have some resemblance to the real world around us, but they are not reality. Our thoughts are endlessly creative, but not inherently meaningful. You decide the meaning of your thoughts.

Emotional Reasoning

This is another version of fusion, and it's when your emotional experience (as opposed to your thoughts) defines your reality. You assume that the presence of a feeling is synonymous with a certain outcome. With emotional reasoning, a feeling ceases to be a potential indicator, but instead becomes a definite predictor. If you're feeling it, then it's real and meaningful. No flexibility, no room for interpretation. For example:

- *If I'm anxious, there must be danger.*

- *If I feel guilty, I must have done something wrong.*

- *If I feel embarrassed, everyone must be judging me.*

- *If something feels incomplete, it must be wrong.*

While feelings can function as an indicator (e.g., anxiety alerting you to danger), it's important to remember that there is always an important asterisk—anxiety means that you *might* be in danger; guilt means that you *might* have done something wrong. Think of it kind of like getting honked at while driving—you may have done something wrong, but it also might be an impatient driver who doesn't understand what "NO TURN ON RED" means. You're going to want to give the situation a quick once-over to determine if that emotional reminder is actually useful.

Fusion with Beliefs

This is another version of fusion in which you get lost in the automatic mental narratives that show up, even though they may not truly align with your beliefs. We all need shortcuts; we need handy mental maps and stories to help us navigate the world more smoothly so that we don't have to start from scratch every time. These beliefs about ourselves and the world around us can be helpful, but they can also get in the way. When we get stuck with a narrative that isn't working, we generally do best to update it or jettison it all together. But sometimes we hold onto it tightly, rigidly adhering to these narratives long after they've shown themselves to be unhelpful. For example:

- *I must always do everything possible to succeed, no matter the cost.*

- *I ought to be better at this.*

- *I should be able to solve this problem.*

- *I have to achieve certainty.*

Outdated beliefs can cause a lot of pain. We often develop our foundational narratives about the world when we're young. But unfortunately, we don't have a great sample size in our youth. The people around us— our parents, siblings, classmates—may not be representative of the rest of the world. Maybe your parents were volatile or hard to please and so you adapted by trying to never make mistakes. Maybe your classmates were mean and so you protected yourself by staying quiet and trying not to upset anyone. These adjustments were useful and adaptive in your circumstances; you found the best way to get through. But at some point, your circumstances changed and you may not have updated your approach. If you avoid mistakes at all costs, you miss the opportunity to learn that mistakes can be tolerable and even helpful. If you are a people-pleaser and avoid conflict at all costs, you miss the opportunity to learn that you can be kind, caring, and a good friend, all while setting boundaries and getting your own needs met too.

Sometimes these obsolete beliefs hang around. It can be frustrating when you have the insight—you see exactly where they came from and why they don't work for you anymore—and yet they still interfere. You intellectually know that it's okay for you to be imperfect, but old habits die hard and you can't quite shake the feeling. This is where defusion can be helpful. By stepping back and seeing the belief, you can give yourself space to make a choice that better aligns with your well-being. You don't need to wait for the resolution of the feeling or for the old belief to subside; you can side-step that process by unsticking from the belief and seeing it for what it is. These rules that you've made for yourself—about your role in the world, how you need to be—are not ironclad. You're not beholden to them and, once you create space to see them as they are, you can make a choice that fits better for you now.

Practicing Defusion

Now for the fun stuff. Enough about fusion; let's get into defusion. You need to get yourself unstuck. You can't stop worrying while you're still melded together with your thoughts. You've become accustomed to responding to your thoughts and feelings as if they have power, like they're a force to be reckoned with. But your thoughts are more like the Wizard of Oz cowering behind his curtain, hoping that you don't figure out the illusion. These parlor tricks can be scary and feel very real when you're immersed, but you can pull back the curtain. Russ Harris, an ACT therapist and trainer, uses a metaphor called "Demons on a Boat" (2008) to describe this process of pulling back the curtain—it's adapted here:

> Imagine that you're out at sea, sailing a boat far from shore. Under the deck of the boat is a hoard of demons. They're awful—massive claws, sharp teeth, rotten breath, horrifying growls. But the demons have made a deal with you: as long as you keep the boat drifting aimlessly out at sea, they'll stay out of your way. They'll remain below deck and you'll be free to go on drifting.
>
> One day you decide to turn the boat back to shore. The demons come flooding out from below deck, gnashing their teeth, growling their growls. And you, terrified, concede and turn the boat back out to sea. As promised, the demons go back below deck and you breathe a sigh of relief.
>
> Over time you start to feel dissatisfied with your life at sea. You're anxious, depressed, bored, lonely. You see other ships heading toward the shore and you summon all of the courage you can and turn your boat around once again. As expected, the demons come flying out from below deck. They threaten and growl and do all of their demon things, but it turns out, that's the extent of their power. They can't touch you. They can't hurt you. All they can do is make a big stink and act scary.

Once you realize that they can't hurt you, the demons are powerless. All of their power lies in intimidation. Your power lies in your ability to accept their presence and see them for what they are. As long as you're willing to allow them to coexist with you and do their demon things, you can steer the boat anywhere you'd like.

Skill Versus Ability

Everyone has the ability to be defused. You do it all the time. These are moments when you're present and connected with the real world around you. You can make decisions, unencumbered by doubt or recriminations. You have moments when you recognize the fallibility of your emotional system and choose to act in accordance with your values rather than kowtow to distress or discomfort. I know you can be defused because you already do it. A whole bunch.

But what you probably don't do enough is build the *skill* of defusion. Blindly stumbling into an outcome is different than intentionally developing the skill to do it well. I know I can successfully shoot a free throw in basketball, but that doesn't necessarily mean I've built the skill to do it consistently. That would take practice and repetition.

When I teach defusion exercises to clients, they sometimes come back saying that they tried, but it "didn't work." They usually mean that their distress didn't go away. Defusion didn't miraculously make their fear or worry instantly evaporate. Well, it's not supposed to. This is a tool to help you relate to your fear or worry in a different way; it's not a tool to change these feelings. Now of course, I would predict that if you relate to these experiences in a more adaptive way, they're likely to dissipate on their own, but that's not your explicit goal. Your goal is to create space so that you can act with more intention. It's to pry you free of the grip of these feelings so that you can retake control—not of the feelings themselves, but of your life. When you are defused, you have the flexibility to live and act independently, without deference to whatever thoughts, feelings, or beliefs rise to the surface in any given moment.

Practice

Given what you know about my middling athletic ability, what do you think would happen if you pulled me off the bench to shoot free throws in the final seconds of the NBA Finals? Sadly, I suspect it wouldn't go very well. If I had spent hours and hours practicing shooting free throws first, that answer might change. The same is true for you and using defusion—if you only attempt to use these skills when you're deep into worry or at the height of panic, it's probably not going to go very well. Start practicing when things are okay. Don't wait for anxiety to be at a 10, try this when anxiety is at a 2. Using these skills when things are hard requires some mastery, but before you can master a skill you need to establish one first. Carve out some time to practice each day. Make it a regular part of your routine. This is not meant to be an emergency de-escalation technique; it's a metacognitive muscle that you're trying to strengthen and hone. If you want to be able to access this skill when times are hard, you'll first need to lay the foundation.

Defusion Exercises

I've included some sample defusion exercises for you to practice. They're broken down into three categories—imaginal, verbal, and physical. Essentially, defusion via thinking, saying, and doing. I'd recommend trying several so as not to get too stuck or rigid with one particular method. These exercises are all a means to the same end: facilitating the process of defusion.

Imaginal

Imagine your thoughts as leaves on a stream, floating into your awareness and back out again as they drift, one by one, through the slowly moving current. Don't hold on to the leaves or try to change their path; simply allow them to trickle through your mind without interference or judgment. As each thought arises, watch it with detachment and let it float merrily along.

Imagine your thoughts as clouds in the sky, lightly drifting through the air. Watch them come and go, simply observing their path through the sky. They may move quickly or slowly. You may notice yourself wanting to change something about how they appear. Acknowledge that desire to change the clouds and relinquish control. Notice that you are not the clouds, but the infinite sky, with plenty of room for thoughts to come and go.

Create a mental scene of your worry thoughts. Hold that scene in your mind, but now transform it by changing the genre. Make it a Western, a slapstick comedy, or sci-fi. Imagine it as directed by Wes Anderson, Michael Bay, or Quentin Tarantino. It could be a commercial, complete with a catchy jingle. Or a cheesy reality show, with cliff-hangers and drama. Notice how your thoughts are pliable. Try making it a theater production—it could be an elaborate Broadway production or a no-frills community theater rendition. The content remains the same, but the context can shift.

Give thanks to your mind for its input. Rather than arguing or resisting, playfully thank your mind for its suggestion—*Thank you, mind, for bringing that thought to my attention. I appreciate the effort to help, but I think I'll go in a different direction.*

Arbitrarily assign the thought to an object. Build defusion by assigning the thought to an object around you. Intentionally think the thought each time you encounter the object, creating a mental association. Notice the arbitrary nature of this association. Bring the object with you (if it's portable), going about your day without avoidance of that thought. Your thought/object can come along for the ride, but it does not need to dictate your behavior.

Verbal

Say out loud: "I notice I'm having the thought that _____."

Say the thought in a funny voice or accent—a robot, Daffy Duck, Cookie Monster, Arnold Schwarzenegger. This is a good opportunity to practice your favorite impressions!

Change the speed in which you say the thought: sound it out slowly, drawing out each sound syllable by syllable; speed it up, like an auctioneer.

Use Google Translate to translate your thought into another language, then say it out loud in that language.

Sing your thoughts to the tune of a song—Happy Birthday, Row, Row, Row Your Boat, etc.

Use sarcasm—"Good one, brain!", "You're really on a roll today!", etc.

Physical

Write "I notice I'm having the thought that _____", then make it into a paper airplane. Or fold it up and put it in your pocket.

Keep a running list of your "greatest hits" of unwanted thoughts. Notice that the stories that show up in your mind are rarely original; they're often a variation on a previous thought or theme. Give song titles to each of the "greatest hits."

Illustrate your thought. You can make it realistic or abstract. Do it in the style of Picasso, Matisse, Dalí. Make it a comic strip or cartoon. See if you can find a way to tinker with it and make it silly.

Make your thought into a newspaper headline. For example, "Local Man Dies, Friendless and Alone, After Making Awkward Joke at Dinner Party."

Write your mind an employment rejection letter. For example, "Thank you for your interest in this position. You have a keen ability to conjure up worry, but at this time we're going to choose to live our life based on values and meaning. Random scary thoughts might be a better fit for another organization. We appreciate your time and wish you the best of luck in your future endeavors."

Defusion Is Experiential

Some of these exercises are silly. Maybe they feel a little hokey or embarrassing. Maybe you bristle at the idea of doing a contrived exercise or you shudder at something so aggressively peaceful as "Leaves on a Stream." I hear you. But the thing is, these tools work if you do them. You can't just read over them and expect to absorb the skill. There's no defusion osmosis. It *must* be done experientially. So get out of your comfort zone a bit. Don't let self-consciousness or judgment get in the way of assembling the toolbox that you need. Practice. Do what you need to do to develop the skills that will help you better manage your worry. If the demons on your boat are self-consciousness or discomfort, be willing to steer your ship toward what matters to you and let the demons come along for the ride.

Coming Up Next...

We're coming to the end! You've learned about anxiety and how it works. You've learned strategies to relate differently to your worry. And now you've learned some exercises to help you to respond more effectively when you feel worried. In the final chapter, we're going to examine traits that will enable you to thrive in spite of worry.

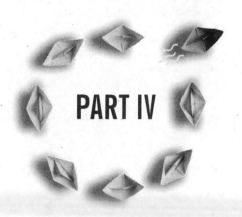

PART IV

Living Unbound
from Worry

CHAPTER TEN

Characteristics of
a Non-Worrier

*The psyche is a polyglot, for if it converts fear into
symptoms it also converts hope.*

—Saul Bellow, *Henderson the Rain King*

Many of the tools described in this book are ways for you to adjust to being someone who worries. They're how you adapt and compensate, knowing that you are already someone who tends to get stuck in their thoughts and feelings. But what are other people out there doing? What about those people who have not needed to compensate or account for worry? Sure, some of that is dumb luck and genetics, but there are also attitudes and practices that can help to insulate you from worry. While the goal is not to be worry-free, there are some things you can learn from the non-worriers. We're going to examine some traits in this chapter that may be helpful in protecting you from the impact of worry. We'll focus on imperfection, self-trust, willingness, and self-compassion.

Imperfection

Are you familiar with the superhuman named Atul Gawande? He's a surgeon at Brigham and Women's Hospital in Boston, MA. And he's also a Harvard professor. And an author of several best-selling books. He's a Rhodes Scholar, he chairs a nonprofit, and he's served in multiple government advisory positions. He also earned two master's degrees, in addition to his MD. And he's a child of immigrants to boot! How on earth does one person do all of these things in one life time?

In his book *Complications: A Surgeon's Notes on an Imperfect Science*, Gawande recounts his experience of grappling with imperfection as a medical student, detailing how he came to accept the reality that mistakes in the field of surgery often meant life or death. He describes a truth that can be uncomfortable to think about—doctors are imperfect. They do their best to *interpret* science and medicine, but they have gaps in their knowledge. They have good days and bad days. They get hungry and tired and grumpy. They have family emergencies and broken garbage disposals and uncooperative children that require mental bandwidth. Like everyone else, they have to make split-second decisions and are susceptible to making mistakes. In fact, in the process of learning to become a doctor, they'll probably make even more mistakes! They will not be a perfect surgeon the first time they perform a surgery. And the ultimate cost of that particular learning curve may even be death.

But what's the alternative? You can watch another surgeon perform a surgery before doing it yourself. You can watch that surgery ten times or a hundred times, but eventually you'll need to do it yourself. And in that moment, you'll be a novice. Without novice surgeons, we never get experienced surgeons. Say goodbye to the field of medicine! This learning curve is not a kink in the system; it's an integral part of it.

I'll come back to my original question: how on earth did Atul Gawande do all of these things? He was able to accept imperfection. He understood that making mistakes is an essential and fundamental part of the process. You don't achieve greatness by accepting only perfection; you achieve it by allowing yourself to be a novice—to feel the pain of costly mistakes, but to use them to grow and do better. These inevitable pitfalls were not deterrents for Gawande, but root parts of the process. Every item on that long list of achievements required that he give himself fully to that process, abandoning the resistance to stumbling along the way.

You can learn to foster a new relationship with perfectionism. It's likely that your desires to find the right answer or to eliminate the possibility of mistakes are at least part of what drives your worrying. Many of my clients try to approach their problem with perfectionism on the fly—they want to implement changes in places where they're already struggling with perfectionism. However, I often suggest that clients start with something more intentional.

Try This for Yourself. Try an activity with the explicit purpose of doing it imperfectly. Approach it with the intention of doing something new for the sake of doing something new. Lean into the discomfort of doing it poorly or not getting it right away. I find that hobbies tend to be a good fit here—try learning a new instrument, signing up for an art class, taking up gardening, woodworking, or baking. The goal is to learn to engage in activities with curiosity and openness rather than with a focus on measurement or achievement. Use these activities as a way to practice openness to being a beginner. I know this exercise is different from some of the others in this book—it's not a quick, five-minute endeavor. To meaningfully incorporate this trait in your life, you'll need to sustain your effort and live a lifestyle conducive to embracing imperfection.

Self-Trust

Inherent in worry is a distrust in yourself. You're unable to trust in your skills and abilities, unwilling to put faith in your instincts or decision-making. Those perfectionistic standards that we just discussed can begin to erode trust in your ability. It can start to feel like anything short of a complete and absolute understanding of a task means that you're ill equipped for that task. For example, many students going off to college lack specific skills to live independently. Maybe they don't know how to do their laundry or navigate the campus bus system. Maybe they don't know where the dining hall is or how to get in touch with their academic advisor. While these are surely problems to be addressed, the goal is not to send every kid off to college knowing exactly how to do everything. That would be an insurmountable goal. No one would ever be fit to leave their parents' home if the prerequisite was a complete mastery of all "adulting" tasks.

The goal of learning every skill is impossibly high, but luckily, we can set a goal that is both more reasonable and more effective. Instead of learning how to do everything, you simply need to learn how to *figure out* how to do everything. I don't need to know how to change my car's transmission—I just need to know how to locate a mechanic. I don't need to know the best route to my doctor's office—I just need to know how to use a mapping app. And most importantly, I don't need to figure out how to do everything well—I am perfectly capable of failing and being okay.

I had a client who had a fear of driving. For him, it wasn't necessarily about the skill of driving itself, but more about the litany of things that could go wrong. All of the what-ifs that were out of his control: drunk drivers, flat tires, clunking sounds, icy roads, you name it! We identified some measures that he could take that might help him to feel more confident, like learning to change a tire. But it was equally important to recognize that he didn't have to know everything. If he did get a flat tire and didn't know how to change one, he could call AAA. Or a local tow company. If he didn't have a phone, well, he could flag someone down or walk to the nearest gas station. Of course, those last options wouldn't be ideal. But "not ideal" is very different from catastrophe. "Not ideal" does not mean that you're bad or wrong or that you can't handle it.

It's often these kinds of unlikely scenarios that generate worry. You get stuck trying to think your way through every scenario—to plan for every possibility while going off to college or driving a car. But you're waaaaay overdoing it. You don't need to hone every skill or anticipate every unlikely event; you only need to develop the basic skills of problem-solving. And then trust in yourself.

To function in the world, we need to make some basic assumptions. We have to trust that things will generally work the way they're supposed to work. I need to assume that the computer I'm typing on isn't going to explode in my face, that the chair I'm sitting in isn't going to spontaneously crumble, that the floor it all rests on isn't going to collapse underneath me. This trust is essential to moving smoothly through the world; without it, I'd be stuck examining everything. You need to put a similar trust in yourself. Trust that you are capable of making reasonable decisions. Trust that you can solve unexpected problems that come your way. This doesn't mean you'll be perfect or that you won't make mistakes, but simply that you'll get reasonable results most of the time.

So how does one become okay with this possibility for mistakes? By *practicing* trust. Think about your friendships and relationships for a moment—how have you built trust in other people? Do you control and scrutinize everything they do to ensure that they won't hurt you? Or do you make yourself vulnerable, knowing that this kind of openness to being hurt is essential to building strong connections? Trust *requires* risk. To build and establish trust in others, we need to give them opportunities to earn our trust. The same is true for ourselves. If you want to learn to trust yourself, you need to get open and vulnerable. You need to allow yourself opportunities to earn it.

Try This for Yourself.
Seek out opportunities to earn your own trust. Find a situation where you can make a quick, fluid decision without analysis. Opt to make the call in a situation where you might have previously sought out reassurance from others. Rather than surfing through Netflix for an hour trying to find the "right" thing, set a timer for a minute and then choose. Rather than reading reviews of twenty different toasters before you buy one, just look at a couple options and take the plunge. Instead of rereading that email to your coworker, just write it and press "send."

And remember, the point is not that you'll love that movie on Netflix or that you'll choose the perfect toaster or that your email to your colleague will be hailed as a great literary work. The point is that you are capable of making reasonable choices. The movie may not be amazing, the toaster will eventually break, and your email may have typos, but you can withstand all of that. You can be trusted to do reasonable things without pouring over each decision.

Willingness

When I worked in residential OCD treatment, there was a client who had an obsession about losing important personal belongings. He would compulsively check over and over again. As you might imagine, when he came to treatment, we encouraged him to eliminate his checking compulsions. And he did. But every day, I'd walk into the program and find him pacing at the bottom of the stairs that led to his room. While he wasn't going up to his room to check, he had also not moved on. He was tormented, white-knuckling his way through the experience. He was still wrestling with it.

Willingness is about making space for your emotional experience. Accepting the presence of uncomfortable feelings or thoughts, but letting go of the struggle and resistance. For the client pacing at the bottom of the stairs, willingness would be more than simply not checking; it would mean allowing those feelings to exist while continuing with his day.

One study conducted at that same residential treatment program (Reid et al. 2017) found that individuals had faster symptom reduction when they had higher degrees of willingness. Willingness doesn't necessarily mean that you like or endorse the experience you're having; it simply means that you've committed to stop fighting it. You're making space for it, rather than trying to suppress it or wish it away.

Try This for Yourself. When you find yourself anxious or worried, pause for a moment and notice what you're feeling. Ask yourself: *Am I willing to have this experience? Can I get more open to it? Can I let go a little bit more?* If you're resisting or struggling with it, see if you can lean into the feeling and practice acceptance of the experience. Soften your stance by getting curious and interested in the feeling. Remember, worrying is often about being *unwilling* to have an experience—being unwilling to feel anxious, uncertain, or unresolved. By practicing willingness, you can remove some of the fuel powering your worry.

Self-Compassion

I have a confession to make: I resisted the idea of self-compassion for a long time. I pride myself on utilizing evidence-based treatment models and I know that I can sometimes unfairly turn up my nose at practices that I deem to have a whiff of pseudoscience. I think this comes from a good place—I've worked with many clients who have been harmed by clinicians who, with good intentions, offer ineffective treatment simply because they don't know any better. Self-compassion, at first, seemed to me like a feel-good positive affirmation, nothing more. Boy, was I wrong. And there is actually a whole body of research to back it up.

Self-compassion has been associated with lower anxiety and depression (Brown et al. 2019), improved tolerance for uncertainty (Deniz 2021), and improved emotional regulation (Finlay-Jones et al. 2015). It's helpful for stress and cognitive fusion (Yadavaia, Hayes, and Vilardaga 2014) and it's correlated with greater life satisfaction (Neff 2003).

What I've grown to better understand and appreciate is that self-compassion is not merely an idea—it's an actual mechanism of change (Keng et al. 2012). It's not just filler—it's an active part of the therapeutic process. Most behavioral models rely on learning—I ask my clients to forego worrying, expecting that they will ultimately learn that they're okay. Nothing bad happened; they were capable of getting through the temporary distress. But what do my clients learn if they forego worrying and then self-flagellate? What happens if they eliminate that extra analysis, but instead beat themselves up? Are they really any better off if, instead of a mind filled with analysis, they're now bombarded with messages like *You're a failure* or *You're irresponsible* or *You shouldn't make mistakes?* Are they actually learning that they're okay? What I've come to realize is that self-compassion is a pivotal part of the learning.

I worked with a client who had OCD and struggled with intrusive thoughts. While we were able to eliminate some of the more overt compulsions fairly quickly, there was still more that was getting in the way. She had stopped performing compulsions, only to be filled with self-hatred. Any time she would catch herself having fun, she'd retreat, believing that she was undeserving of joy. Basic acts of self-care—showering, eating, spending time with people—were treated as an unearned indulgence. She lived largely in isolation, cut off from the things that brought meaning and purpose to her life. While this may be a more drastic presentation, many people find themselves in similar situations. Without worrying, they feel unfit for the world. To make a mistake, to falter, would be unforgivable.

For this client struggling to give herself permission to merely exist in the world, we had to pivot our focus. Treatment was no longer about resisting compulsions, but instead, it became about practicing care for herself. Being kind to herself was an active part of the treatment. It was an essential component that was required in order for her to learn what she needed to learn: That she was okay—even without compulsions, even without self-flagellation. No strings attached. Her worth and her right to take up space in the world were not contingent on being perfect or avoiding mistakes. She could go out into the world, blemishes and all, and still practice treating herself with positive regard.

Kristen Neff, a researcher and champion of self-compassion, identifies three components of self-compassion practice (2003): self-kindness, common humanity, and mindfulness.

Self-kindness (versus self-judgment). What do you do when you make a mistake? How do you respond to moments of pain, inadequacy, or failure? Practicing self-kindness means that you take a non-judgmental stance. You give yourself warmth and understanding. For me, parenting has helped clarify what self-compassion looks like because nine times out of ten, the compassionate response is the one I want to offer to my kids. If they fall off their bike, my response is not, "You suck! You should be better at riding your bike;" it's, "That looks like it hurts. It can be hard to learn new things. It's really cool that you're trying." My goal is to support them by fostering an environment in which they can feel safe in trying new things, making mistakes, and knowing that they'll be loved whether or not they nail it. And believe it or not, as adults, we need the same things. We need kindness and empathy. Self-criticism and judgment do not foster growth—they stifle it. They don't hold us accountable; they ensure that we'll experience shame when we inevitably face imperfection. Self-kindness merely means that we take responsibility for fostering our own environment in which we can grow. We offer care and understanding because that's what human beings need to thrive.

Common humanity (versus isolation). It can be easy to take things personally sometimes. After all, you have a vested interest in you. But as unique as you are, your experience of pain and suffering is not special. You're not flawed or cursed. You're not alone in your struggles. Everyone feels pain. Everyone is connected in their clunky, mess of a life. Making mistakes, experiencing adversity, and even failure are all parts of the shared human experience. By acknowledging this common humanity, you can extend yourself some empathy. Recognition that your pain is a normal and necessary part of life, not a flaw or exception, can allow you to put your challenges into perspective. Life difficulties do not happen only to you; they are part of what connects you to all of the people around you.

Mindfulness (versus over-identification). To extend compassion to yourself and the feelings you experience, you must first allow yourself room to feel those emotions, to be the observer of your inner experience. By mindfully holding your thoughts and feelings in balanced perspective, you can make space for them without becoming immersed. When we over-identify with those internal experiences—that is, we put too much stock in our passing thoughts or feelings—we lose our ability to respond effectively. Chapter 9 covered this idea at length, so we won't go into much detail here. But mindful recognition of your present moment is a first step toward treating yourself more kindly and connecting with common humanity.

Applying Self-Compassion

Now that we've discussed the benefits of self-compassion and explored what it can look like, we're going to detail a few exercises that can help build the habit of self-compassion. Remember, knowing that you should be more compassionate with yourself and actually doing it are two very different things. You have to practice!

Ideal Compassionate Figures

One way to offer yourself compassion is to channel another person. This could be someone in your life—perhaps a person who has shown you unconditional love—or a fictional character who embodies the three aspects of self-compassion. For me, it's Gandalf from *Lord of the Rings*. He feels deeply, but remains focused on what's important (mindfulness). He acknowledges the quiet dignity of even the smallest or seemingly insignificant creatures, recognizing that their flaws do not negate their inherent worth (common humanity). He doesn't beat himself up for not realizing that the One Ring was right under his nose for decades, and he values a good smoke with his friends (self-kindness). Some other classics that I've heard over the years: Yoda, Dumbledore, Jesus, Atticus Finch, Mary Poppins, Charlotte (of *Charlotte's Web*), and Mister Rogers.

To channel your ideal compassionate figure, imagine what they might say to you if they were right there with you. How would they talk to you? What would they say? Would they be accepting of you? Or judgmental? Would they offer love and acknowledgment? Or criticism and rejection? What would it be like if this person were there with you all the time to offer this compassion? See if you can practice talking to yourself in this way.

Talking to a Friend

I'm often amazed at how compassionate my clients can be to the people around them, and how much they struggle to extend that same courtesy to themselves. Using whatever problem you're dealing with, see if you can imagine what you might say to a good friend or loved one who was struggling with that issue. How does it differ from how you talk to yourself about this issue? Would you ever dream of talking to a friend in the way that you talk to yourself? Why would that harsh criticism be acceptable for you but not for them? Try to extend to yourself the same care and compassion that you demonstrate to others.

Self-Compassion Journal

Like many practices in this book, self-compassion is a habit that you have to build. To get to a point where you may be able to integrate self-compassion more seamlessly into your life, you may benefit from starting with a more intentional practice. Try a self-compassion journal. Take some time at the end of each day to write about an experience where you struggled. Maybe you were short with a loved one or you made a mistake at work. Incorporating the three components of self-compassion (self-kindness, common humanity, and mindfulness), see if you can practice a different response to the experience.

For example, if I made a mistake at work, my journal entry might look like this: *I felt angry with myself when I was late to a meeting. I care about being punctual and want people to feel that I value their time, but I know that we all make mistakes. Everyone is late sometimes. It's okay that I messed up.*

Or, if I got irritated with a loved one: *I got mad today when my kids weren't listening. I yelled at them and then felt ashamed that I had not parented in the way that I intended. Parenting is hard and no one makes it through without sometimes losing their cool. It's understandable that I might feel angry. It's okay to feel upset and disappointed.*

Wrapping Up

We've covered a lot of ground in this book. Hopefully you've come to know your own worry a bit more intimately and figured out what's making it tick. I hope you've found some strategies that fit your proprietary blend of worrying and that you can start putting these into practice.

Be patient with yourself. You'll inevitably make mistakes. You'll catch yourself reverting to old habits. That's all perfectly understandable. It's all part of the process of learning new things. Know that it will take time before these skills start to feel more intuitive. Allow yourself space to be a novice. There may be a time when these new strategies feel like second nature, when they become effortless. But you also may find that they continue to take work. Neither of these outcomes is bad or wrong. It's okay if it's hard for you. Whether you completely eliminate worrying from your repertoire or continue to slip into it from time to time, the important part is that you're engaged in the process and fostering a relationship with your mind that allows you to grow and thrive.

Acknowledgments

To my countless clients over the years, whose bravery and strength have inspired me and whose wisdom is contained in the pages of this book. I am privileged to have been part of your journey and grateful for you to be part of mine.

To my team at New Harbinger—Jennye Garibaldi, Vicraj Gill, and Joyce Wu. Your expert guidance, excitement for this project, and patience with a first-time author have been indispensable.

To my friends and former colleagues at McLean Hospital's OCD Institute, whose compassion, skill, and ingenuity have set a high bar and provided a shining example of the clinician that I aspire to be. Your care and devotion to the OCD community are lifesaving and have left me without a doubt that I have found my professional place.

To Mom, Dad, and Dan—your endless support and encouragement have been invaluable. Thanks for fostering a spirit of curiosity and life-long learning. It's meant the world to me to have you in my corner.

To Harper, Marlowe, Owen, and Zoey—your excitement, your goofiness, your tears, and your joy all remind me how lucky I am to be in a world brimming with purpose. Thanks for making our days messy but beautiful and packed to the gills with life.

To Becca—your love, support, and willingness to watch four kids while I write on the weekends make everything possible. Thank you for being the best companion and building this life together. You're still the only person I never get tired of.

References

Baker, A., M. Mystkowski, N. Culver, R. Yi, A. Mortazavi, and M. Craske. 2010. "Does Habituation Matter: Emotional Processing Theory and Exposure Therapy for Acrophobia." *Behaviour Research and Therapy* 48(11): 1139–43.

Bailey, R., and A. Wells. 2015. "Metacognitive Beliefs Moderate the Relationship Between Catastrophic Misinterpretation and Health Anxiety." *Journal of Anxiety Disorders* 34: 8–14.

Baumeister, R., K. Vohs, and D. Tice. 2007. "The Strength Model of Self-Control." *Current Directions in Psychological Science* 16(6): 351–5.

Brown, S., M. Hughes, S. Campbell, and M. Cherry. 2020. "Could Worry and Rumination Mediate Relationships Between Self-Compassion and Psychological Distress in Breast Cancer Survivors?" *Clinical Psychology & Psychotherapy* 27(1): 1–10.

Cartwright-Hatton, S., and A. Wells. 1997. "Beliefs About Worry and Intrusions: The Meta-Cognitions Questionnaire and Its Correlates." *Journal of Anxiety Disorders* 11(3): 279–96.

Collardeau, F., B. Corbyn, J. Abramowitz, P. Janssen, S. Woody, and N. Fairbrother. 2019. "Maternal Unwanted and Intrusive Thoughts of Infant-Related Harm, Obsessive-Compulsive Disorder and Depression in the Perinatal Period." *BMC Psychiatry* 19(1): 94.

Deniz, M. 2021. "Self-Compassion, Intolerance of Uncertainty, Fear of COVID-19, and Well-Being: A Serial Mediation Investigation." *Personality and Individual Differences* 177: 110824.

Dweck, C. 2007. *Mindset: The New Psychology of Success.* New York: Ballantine Books.

Finlay-Jones, A., C. Rees, and R. Kane. 2015. "Self-Compassion, Emotional Regulation, and Stress Among Australian Psychologists: Testing an Emotion Regulation Model of Self-Compassion Using Structural Equation Modeling." *PLoS ONE* 10(7): e0133481.

Gawande, A. 2003. *Complications: A Surgeon's Notes on an Imperfect Science.* New York: Picador.

Harris, R. 2008. *The Happiness Trap: How to Stop Struggling and Start Living.* Boston: Trumpeter Publishing.

Hazlett-Stevens, H., B. Zucker, and M. Craske. 2002. "The Relationship of Thought-Action Fusion to Pathological Worry and Generalized Anxiety Disorder." *Behaviour Research and Therapy* 40(10): 1199–204.

Keng, S., M. Smoski, C. Robins, A. Ekblad, and J. Brantley. 2012. "Mechanisms of Change in Mindfulness-Based Stress Reduction: Self-Compassion and Mindfulness as Mediators of Intervention Outcomes." *Journal of Cognitive Psychotherapy* 26(3): 270–80.

McGonigal, K. 2013. *The Willpower Instinct: How Self-Control Works, Why It Matters, and What You Can Do to Get More of It*. New York: Avery Publishing.

McKay, D. 2006. "Treating Disgust Reactions in Contamination-Based Obsessive-Compulsive Disorder." *Journal of Behavior Therapy and Experimental Psychiatry* 37(1): 53–9.

Neff, K. 2003. "The Development and Evaluation of a Scale to Measure Self-Compassion." *Self and Identity* 2(3): 223–50.

Neff, K., K. Kirkpatrick, and S. Rude. 2007. "Self-Compassion and Adaptive Psychological Functioning." *Journal of Research in Personality* 41(1): 139–54.

O'Connor, K., and F. Aardema. 2011. *Clinician's Handbook for Obsessive Compulsive Disorder: Inference-Based Therapy*. West Sussex, UK: Wiley-Blackwell.

Olafiranye, O., G. Jean-Louis, F. Zizi, J. Nunes, and M. Vincent. 2011. "Anxiety and Cardiovascular Risk: Review of Epidemiological and Clinical Evidence." *Mind and Brain: The Journal of Psychiatry* 2(1): 32–7.

Rachman, S., and P. de Silva. 1978. "Abnormal and Normal Obsessions." *Behavior Research and Therapy* 16(4): 233–48.

Reid, A., L. Garner, N. Van Kirk, C. Gironda, J. Krompinger, B. Brennan, et al. 2017. "How Willing Are You? Willingness as a Predictor of Change During Treatment of Adults with Obsessive-Compulsive Disorder." *Depression and Anxiety* 34(11): 1057–64.

Shafran, R., D. Thordarson, and S. Rachman. 1996. "Thought-Action Fusion in Obsessive Compulsive Disorder." *Journal of Anxiety Disorders* 10(5): 379–91.

Thompson-Hollands, J., T. Farchione, and D. Barlow. 2013. "Thought-Action Fusion Across Anxiety Disorder Diagnoses: Specificity and Treatment Effects." *Journal of Nervous and Mental Disease* 201(5): 407–13.

Vigen, T. 2015. *Spurious Correlations*. New York: Hachette Books.

Wells, A. 2011. *Metacognitive Therapy for Anxiety and Depression*. New York: Guilford Press.

Wells, A., and C. Carter. 2001. "Further Tests of a Cognitive Model of Generalized Anxiety Disorder: Metacognition and Worry in GAD, Panic Disorder, social Phobia, Depression, and Nonpatients." *Behavior Therapy* 32(1): 85–102.

Yadavaia, J., S. Hayes, and R. Vilardaga. 2014. "Using Acceptance and Commitment Therapy to Increase Self-Compassion: A Randomized Control Trial." *Journal of Contextual Behavioral Science* 3(4): 248–57.

Ben Eckstein, LCSW, is owner and director of Bull City Anxiety & OCD Treatment Center in Durham, NC. Eckstein was trained at McLean Hospital's OCD Institute, and has been specializing in the treatment of anxiety and obsessive-compulsive disorder (OCD) for over a decade. He serves on the board of directors for OCD North Carolina, and offers training, workshops, and speaking engagements in addition to his clinical work.

Foreword writer **Lisa W. Coyne, PhD**, is founder and senior clinical consultant of the McLean OCD Institute for Children and Adolescents (OCDI Jr.), and assistant professor in the department of psychiatry at Harvard Medical School. She founded and directs the New England Center for OCD and Anxiety.

MORE BOOKS from
NEW HARBINGER PUBLICATIONS

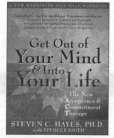

Did you know there are **free tools** you can download for this book?

Free tools are things like **worksheets, guided meditation exercises**, and **more** that will help you get the most out of your book.

You can download free tools for this book— whether you bought or borrowed it, in any format, from any source—from the New Harbinger website. All you need is a NewHarbinger.com account. Just use the URL provided in this book to view the free tools that are available for it. Then, click on the "download" button for the free tool you want, and follow the prompts that appear to log in to your NewHarbinger.com account and download the material.

You can also save the free tools for this book to your **Free Tools Library** so you can access them again anytime, just by logging in to your account! Just look for this button on the book's free tools page.

+ Save this to my free tools library

If you need help accessing or downloading free tools, visit **newharbinger.com/faq** or contact us at **customerservice@newharbinger.com**.